Helping Children Care for God's People

200 Ideas for Teaching Stewardship and Mission

Delia Halverson

Abingdon Press
Nashville

Helping Children Care for God's People:
200 Ideas for Teaching Mission and Stewardship

Copyright © 1994 by Abingdon Press

This book is printed on acid-free, recycled paper.

Library of Congress Cataloging-in-Publication Data

Halverson, Delia Touchton.
  Helping children care for God's people:200 ideas for teaching mission and stewardship/Delia Halverson.
    p.   cm.
  ISBN 0-687-41103-3 (pbk.:alk. paper)
  1. Missions—Study and teaching (Elementary)   2. Stewardship, Christian—Study and teaching (Elementary)   I. Title.
BV2090.5.H35   1994
268'.432—dc20   94-15769

Scripture quotations are from the New Revised Standard Version Bible, Copyright 1989 by the Division of Christian Education of the National Council of the Churches of Christ in the USA. Used by permission.

"It's Not My Job!" by DeAnne Trujillo is reprinted by permission from *Upper-Elementary Meetings*, Copyright 1989. Published by Group Publishing, Inc., Box 481, Loveland, CO 80539.

"The Jug of Water" is reprinted from *Stories for Telling* by William R. White, copyright © Augsburg Publishing House. Used by permission of Augsburg Fortress.

Apology to Native Congregations, "Gathering into the Sacred Circle," of the *Whole People of God Curriculum*, Unit 1, is used by permission of The United Church of Canada.

"I Have a Dream" by Amy Thandiwe Globedale is from *Skipping Stones*, A Multicultural Children's Quarterly Journal, P.O. Box 3939, Eugene OR 97403. Used by permission.

The words of the song "Did You Ever See a Steward" by Sarah Fletcher are from *Stewardship: Taking Care of God's World*, Copyright 1984 Concordia Publishing House. Used by permission.

94 95 96 97 98 99 00 01 02 03 04—10 9 8 7 6 5 4 3 2 1

MANUFACTURED IN THE UNITED STATES OF AMERICA

To
my parents,
Paul and Edith Touchton,
and my sister,
Mary Jewell Touchton Atkins,
and all those
who lived with us in
The Touchton International House

Through those experiences,
I learned
to care for God's people.

Contents

Stewardship and Mission, Hand in Hand

It was Wednesday night, and as I drove away from the church, I smugly thought of our Wednesday experiences. What a delightful program we had for our children! What a joy it was to minister to children, sharing learning experiences, fellowship, food, and fun. Then it suddenly hit me. Our children were only on the receiving end. They had nothing to do with the planning, and they had no real opportunities to give to others, except an occasional gift made during craft time. All forty or so adults gave of their talents each week, but we gave our children only the opportunity to receive. How could they be good stewards of their talents and experience the joy of giving to and doing for others, if we didn't personally involve them in mission?

Stewardship and mission are the head and feet of ministry. You can't have one without the other! Stewardship tells us what, how, and why we must be in mission, and the outreach of mission is impossible without the time, talents, and money that we, God's stewards, can offer.

Because most churches have separate committees or departments for stewardship and mission, educators usually ignore these arteries of our Christian life and thereby miss golden opportunities. Oh sure, we teach occasional sessions on these themes from our curriculum, and once a year we mention the "stewardship campaign" or encourage participation in a week of mission study. But we fail to plug into the many other experiences that bring this joy in Christian living to ourselves and to our children. We must teach our children "habits of the heart."

Defining Mission and Stewardship

My mother told me that as a child, she wanted to be a missionary, but she worried that she would not grow up fast enough, that all the mission work would be accomplished! Most of us have a very limited idea of missions. We think of missions as something that happens in a far country, or perhaps someplace else in our country. In reality, our mission is what God calls us to do. We do not respond to that call in order to receive God's love, but *because* we receive it. God freely gives love unconditionally. That love (or grace) always stands available, and we cannot earn it. But when we accept God's love, we respond in mission. This is our way of returning God's love. As Jesus said,

> "The first [commandment] is, 'Hear O Israel: the Lord our God, the Lord is one; you shall love the Lord your God with all your heart, and with all your soul, and with all your mind, and with all your strength.' The second is this, 'You shall love your neighbor as yourself.' There is no other commandment greater than these." *(Mark 12:29-31)*

In John 15:12-17, Jesus challenges us to live in love for one another. He sets us aside, appoints us to bear the fruit of his message. At the end of the book of Matthew, Jesus gives us the great commission:

"Go therefore and make disciples of all nations, baptizing them in the name of the Father and of the Son and of the Holy Spirit, and teaching them to obey everything that I have commanded you. And remember, I am with you always, to the end of the age." *(Matt. 28:19-20)*

We act in mission . . .

    . . . when we tell someone else about our Sunday school class;

    . . . when we hug a friend who is sad;

    . . . when we take a plate of cookies to a sick friend.

Mission is our response to God's urging and to God's love. As we act in mission, we say thank you to God.

We also limit our idea of stewardship. Often we look at stewardship only as giving money. Ask a group of children to define a steward, and you are likely to hear from at least one child that a steward is a person who serves food and drinks on an airplane. Ask most adults in the church to define the function of the stewardship committee, and they probably will tell you that it raises money to meet the budget. Both these definitions are right, but stewardship encompasses a much broader concept. A steward actually manages the affairs of another. Well-to-do persons in the past had stewards who managed their households or estates.

The Christian acts as steward of all of God's affairs on earth—in fact, in the universe. To enable us to accomplish this work, God gives us abilities and talents. In I Corinthians 12, Paul reminds us of our gifts, and in Romans 12:1-8 he reminds us that we must all work together, because each of us holds an important role in our mission for Christ.

Our abilities and talents help us, as stewards, to manage the earth, and our health, property, time, and relationships with others. God also gave us the Good News, which tells of Jesus Christ and God's constant love. Stewardship of the Good News calls us into a mission of caring for others, and of sharing the gospel of God's constant love with them. We must manage our talents and put them to work in God's mission, or we lose them. In I Peter 4:10, we read, "Like good stewards of the manifold grace of God, serve one another with whatever gift each of you has received."

God's Gift of Life

Stewardship reaches back into our biblical tradition. God gave us the care of the earth and all that is in it, from the ozone to the starving child. God took a formless void and made the earth, shaping it and giving life to everything in it, according to plan.

Then God said, "Let us make humankind in our image, according to our likeness; and let them have dominion over the fish of the sea, and over the birds of the air, and over the cattle, and over all the wild animals of the earth, and over every creeping thing that creeps upon the earth." *(Gen. 1:26)*

God created everything, and we would not exist if we were not a part of God's plan. That plan includes all of God's creation over which we are given dominion. But the interesting part of this verse is our creation *in God's image*. As created in God's image, our dominion over the earth must take on the character of God. We must function, as stewards, in a loving, caring way.

Nowhere in the Bible does it say that we own the earth or the creatures and people of the earth. We do not have authority to destroy the earth or the personalities of the people, or to use them as we wish. In the true meaning of the word *dominion*, God entrusted us with the earth and everything in it. We are stewards.

In fact, Psalm 24:1 tells us that "The earth is the LORD's and all that is in it, the world, and those who live in it." Psalm 50:10-12 also clearly states that the earth belongs to the Lord, and in Genesis 9, we read that God made a covenant not only with Noah and his family, but also with every living creature. Leviticus 25:23 tells us that we are only tenants of the earth. In this sense, we have responsibility; we are stewards of the earth and all who live in it. The way we care for the earth affects not only us, but all the people and creatures on God's earth, and all those who will follow us.

Christ's Challenge

The three stories that Jesus told in Matthew 25 deal with our responsibility as stewards, and with our mission, or call, to care for God's people. Jesus tells of ten bridesmaids—five who took their responsibilities seriously, and five who ignored their stewardship responsibilities. His second story tells of how three servants used their talents—two followed their master's character and invested their gifts according to their understanding of the master's choice, and one left his gift unused, hiding it in the ground. God gives us opportunities and abilities, and expects us to use them for God's glory.

In the same chapter, immediately following these two stories about our responsibility, we find a story that deals with our call of mission to others. In no uncertain terms, Christ challenges us to reach out to others, to follow God's call: "Truly I tell you, just as you did it to one of the least of these who are members of my family, you did it to me" (25:40).

Many people before us have taken Christ's words seriously. In Acts 8, Luke tells of Philip's trip into Samaria, and how he shared the gospel with the Ethiopian eunuch along the road from Jerusalem to Gaza. In Acts 10:1-35, Peter had a vision that helped him recognize that the church's mission should extend beyond cultural and national boundaries, and Paul and Barnabas were sent on their first mission trip by the church at Antioch (Acts 13:2-3).

Down through the years, we find a rich heritage, filled with those who used their talents and spread God's message of love in their own towns and throughout the world. We continue that tradition today by giving, by participating in volunteer missions, by organizing relief committees, and by caring for one another. Down through the years and into the future, stewardship and mission go hand in hand.

Though created in God's image, we are given wills of our own. God did not make us puppets. We must choose whether to develop the character of God in our own lives, to align ourselves with God, so that we can act as stewards and caring people.

As teachers of children, we face this challenge: We must balance learning about stewardship with the opportunity to serve in mission, to help children learn to care for God's people and God's world.

Suggested Scriptures

You may find the following scriptures useful as you help children care for God's people. Check your concordance under such topics as *love*, *mercy*, *justice*, *neighbor*, *friend*, *peace*, *serve*, and *forgive*, for additional references.

Genesis 1, 2, 8, 9, 13, 41 (*God's gift of earth and how we care*)
Leviticus 25 (*God's gift of earth and how we care*)
Deuteronomy 8, 15, 26 (*God's gift of earth and how we care*)
Ruth (*Caring for others*)
I Kings 17:1-16 (*Widow and son share with Elijah*)
Psalm 8:6 (*Stewards of earth*)
Psalm 24:1 (*God owns all things*)
Psalm 34:13-14 (*Do good/seek peace*)
Psalm 50:10-11, 12b (*God owns all things*)
Psalm 106:1-3; 48 (*Happy are those who observe justice*)
Psalm 133:1 (*Good to live together in unity*)
Proverbs 17:17a (*To be a friend, we always love*)
Isaiah 35:3 (*Make others strong*)
Jeremiah 29:7 (*Seek welfare of community*)
Ezekiel 18:4 (*God owns all things*)
Micah 4:3 (*Swords into plowshares; spears into pruning hooks*)
Haggai 2:8 (*God owns all things*)
Matthew 2:1-12 (*People from other countries worshiped Jesus*)
Matthew 5:43-44 (*Love enemies*)
Matthew 6:24 (*Doing good with our money*)
Matthew 20:26-28 (*Whoever wishes to be great must be servant*)
Matthew 22:37-40 (*Love God/neighbor*)
Matthew 25:14-30 (*Parable of talents*)
Matthew 25:31-46 (*"As you did it to the least of these . . . you did it to me."*)
Matthew 28:19-20 (*Share God's word*)
Mark 2:1-12 (*Jesus heals paralytic*)
Mark 10:29-31 (*First shall be last/last first*)
Mark 12:29-31 (*Love God/neighbor*)
Mark 16:15 (*Proclaim Good News to all the world*)
Luke 8:16-18 (*Don't hide lamp/talent under jar*)
Luke 10:25-37 (*Good Samaritan*)
Luke 12:13-21 (*Jesus and the rich fool*)
Luke 12:31-34 (*Doing good with our money*)
Luke 15:11-32 (*Parable of forgiving father*)
Luke 16:13 (*We cannot serve God and wealth*)
Luke 19:1-10 (*Zacchaeus*)
Luke 19:11-27 (*Parable of the talents*)
John 4:1-42 (*Jesus/person of another culture*)
John 6:1-15 (*Boy shares loaves and fish*)
John 12:23-26 (*Serving God*)
John 13:1-20 (*Jesus serves by washing feet*)
John 13:12-15 (*Follow Jesus/serve others*)
John 14:15-17 (*Share God's word*)
John 15:12-17 (*Love one another*)
John 20:21 (*Peace be with you*)
Acts 1:8 (*Witness to end of earth*)
Acts 2:1-13 (*Holy Spirit comes to disciples from many countries*)

Acts 13:2-3 (*Paul and Barnabas sent on first mission*)
Acts 15:1-35 (*Accepting another without reservation*)
Romans 12:1-8 (*Each has important mission*)
I Corinthians 12 (*We all have talents*)
I Corinthians 13 (*Love chapter*)
II Corinthians 13:11 (*Agree with one another/live in peace*)
Galatians 5:13 (*Through love become slaves to one another*)
Ephesians 4:1-6 (*One body and one spirit*)
Ephesians 4:32 (*Love others and forgive*)
Philippians 2:13 (*God acts in us*)
I Thessalonians 5:15 (*Do good to one and all*)
Hebrews 13:20-21 (*God acts in us*)
James 2:15-16 (*God owns all things*)
I Peter 3:8-9 (*Unity in spirit/Do not repay evil for evil*)
I Peter 4:10 (*Serve with our talents*)
I Peter 5:2-4 (*Do not lord it over others*)
I John 3:17 (*Helping others is more important than money*)
I John 4:7-8 (*Love one another*)

A Child's Understanding

2 After accepting our challenge to help children learn to care for God's people, how do we take the next step? First and foremost, we must act as examples. Then we must understand our children, how they learn, and what concepts they can grasp at particular ages. And certainly, we must develop a plan of action, incorporating stewardship and mission into all aspects of our classroom.

Mentors in Mission

Recently I acted as a mentor in the confirmation program at my church. Requirements for the program included participation in a mission project with my confirmand. We selected ECHO (Educational Concerns for Hunger Organization) as our project. This organization uses volunteer help to research, develop, and distribute seeds and information on trees, edible plants, and small animals to deprived countries. Our hours of digging weeds helped the staff carry out their program. We also had an opportunity to enjoy some of the goats, rabbits, and ducks used to teach food production methods to interns before they leave to work in deprived countries.

I was identified as a "mentor," but we must recognize that we mentor our children even when we never use such a label. Children need to recognize stewardship as a part of our life-style, so a sharing and caring life-style is essential as we mentor our children. Consider hospitality as a foundation for mission. By our actions, we prepare children to think of and reach out to others.

Children catch excitement about caring for God's people. They recognize the way we use our time and talents, and the value we place on the earth and on our material possessions. As adults, we share a responsibility to exhibit and set circumstances that witness to stewardship and create excitement about caring for God's people. Although we may be discouraged with developments in our world, we must drop the attitude of "there goes the neighborhood" and embrace an attitude of "going out to greet the world." As our world comes to our back door through television and magazines, set an example for children by looking with excitement toward learning about new places and new friends. Reach out to our expanding world with joy and anticipation for new opportunities and experiences!

Language

Be conscious of the language you use with children. We adults grew up with phrases and terms that can have negative connotations in today's world. We also used inappropriate generalizations in songs and stories. We read about natives who shot arrows or the "round and fat Eskimo." Occasionally even today, we may find stories that present other countries or their customs as "odd."

Be aware of the way we use colors to suggest negative values. Avoid using such terms as "black sheep" or "black mark" or "yellow-bellied," because of the signals such terms send about various races. Although we don't intend it, these words can hurt. Biblical language used "darkness," rather than "black" in reference to a time when evil things were done in secret. Where possible, describe a specific situation. Use "black" or "white" only to describe actual color, not as a metaphor for extremes of good and evil. Gently correct children who use these terms, suggesting better, more positive words.

Even some of our modern terms or slang phrases send negative signals. What do we tell others when we speak of the "first world" or the "third world"? Does this say that living in the "first world" makes us better? What do we call citizens of the United States? or of Canada? or Brazil or Mexico? By referring to citizens of the United States as "Americans," are we saying that those from Canada, Brazil, and Mexico are not Americans? They also live in America. Words help to shape children in their formative years. Young children often believe that their teachers are always right.

The "Foreign" Image

Look for books and stories that present a true picture of contemporary life in other countries. *Galimoto* by Karen Lynn Williams (New York: Mulberry Books, 1990) is such a book. The story takes place in a contemporary African village, and the illustrations show children as they dress today. At times, you may want to recognize cultural dress, but if the people normally wear western-style clothing, be certain to emphasize the cultural clothing as part of their heritage and state that they wear it on special occasions.

Until recently, people in the United States lived a relatively isolated life. Everything outside our country was "foreign." We labeled customs different from the Anglo-Saxon heritage as foreign, even when practiced by U.S. citizens. Today nothing is foreign, in the true physical sense. The world is in our living rooms through television. We are learning the difference between and the importance of both *multicultural education*, which emphasizes our differences, and *global awareness*, which sees other cultures as related to ours and stresses similarities. Gradually, we learn to see ourselves through the eyes of others.

At one time, we referred to missions as either home missions or foreign missions. In fact, even the methods used to spread the gospel to people of other cultures have changed. In the past, we seemed to feel that in order for people to accept the message of Christ, they must first accept our western culture. This runs completely contrary to biblical teachings. Jesus simply presented his message of love to people of all cultures (see John 4:1-42). Never did he tell them that they must accept his cultural practices—simply accept God's love. Paul fought for the right of Gentiles to accept the message without needing to embrace the Hebrew custom of circumcision (see Acts 15:1-35). Today, when people work with another ethnic group, they first learn about the local culture and then adapt their own lives and teachings to that culture. We no longer "put down" another's way of living.

In the Classroom

The physical surroundings of the classroom also send signals. Are the chairs set up in rows, facing the front, or are they in a circle or in groups, so that children have the opportunity to see faces and interact with one another? If chairs only face the front, we set the teacher up as "authority," giving individual opinions little importance. How can we expect children to care for others, if we give them no opportunity to interact among themselves?

Do the pictures and decorations in the classroom help children appreciate our differences? Search your church files for pictures of the same Bible story as portrayed by various artists. Tell children that we have no real photographs of that day, so different people painted according to the way they imagined the story. Ask them to add their own paintings to the collection, then celebrate the variety of ways the story can be seen. Try to find pictures that show influences of various ethnic backgrounds. I am glad that Jesus came to earth before there were cameras, so that we can picture him with various cultural characteristics.

How does your room or your class procedure show caring? Is the room cheerful and welcoming? Is there someone always on hand to welcome the children? When a visitor comes to your class, how do you introduce the person? Is someone assigned to show him or her around for the first few weeks?

Your stewardship of the earth also speaks through your classroom. Look at your classroom ecology. Consider asking each child to bring a reusable glass or cup from home for snacks, and take turns washing these each time. If this is not possible, at least change to paper cups that can be recycled.

Practice other recycling in your classroom. Keep a box for recycled paper, and always use both sides before throwing it away or putting it in the box. Some cities have recycling services for office paper. Arrange for your church to participate in such a program. Save bits of construction paper and other items for crafts. Mention to the class any time you use recycled items.

Melt crayon pieces to make large rounds of recycled crayons for rubbings and coloring large areas. To do this, oil an old muffin tin and place old crayons (with the paper removed) in the cups. Place the pan in a 250-degree oven and watch carefully as the crayons melt. They also may be melted by placing the crayons in a tin can and setting the can in simmering water on the stove or in an electric fry pan. Then pour the wax into a form to harden. Just remember to be cautious of the hot wax.

Use recycled materials in the classroom not apologetically, but rather with pride. This teaches others to think in similar ways and also fosters throught and discussion about our throwaway culture.

Your attitude teaches children the difference between "needs" and "wants." We have some basic needs and many wants. Perhaps we use the word *need* too often. Do we *need* a glue stick, or is that something we *want* because of its convenience? What other ways can we carry on the same project without using our expensive or ecologically unsound "wants"? Remember that we teach most by our own example.

Understanding Our Children

The way you treat your children teaches them that each of us is an individual, and our differentness is OK. We differ in our physical characteristics, in our personalities, and in our likes and dislikes. But we naturally desire for others to be "like us." That affirms the choices we make and boosts us up. Often, when we differ from someone, we try to build ourselves up by putting down the differentness of another.

A few years ago, several of the adults in our church realized that the children frequently used put-downs both with their peers and with adults. This seemed an accepted pattern. Surprisingly, we discovered that the children did not recognize put-downs and the effect that such statements had on others. We launched a successful campaign to "put down put-downs" and turn frowns into smiles. The results spread even into the public schools, when our children asked permission to post some of their signs and slogans in the classrooms. Be alert to actions of the children in your care and any negative changes you see, even subtle changes.

During a visit to my sister, who is a pediatrician, our daughter (then age two) became ill. My sister asked whether the child normally fell asleep quietly or actively moved about her bed before falling asleep. It occurred to me that I really didn't know my daughter as well as I should. I usually put her in her bed and left the room, and I could not say whether she was active or not before falling asleep. We can easily become lulled into unawareness. With no major problems to alert us, we simply go our way, accepting the way things are as normal.

We often observe children only in relation to the way they affect us or our teaching plan. *Watch* your children and learn. Learn *from* the children, and learn *about* their individual learning patterns.

As you work with your curriculum, you will find opportunities to help children recognize ways they can be stewards and share in God's mission. Your students will learn to recognize themselves as children of God and as disciples of Christ. They will gain skills in relationships with other people. And in your curriculum, you can find opportunities for reaching out to others in love.

Goals for Children

Children's readiness to be in mission and their understanding of stewardship develop gradually as they mature. You can expect different understandings at various ages. A knowledge of age-level understandings of stewardship and mission will enable you to expand on the curriculum and emphasize opportunities to care for God's people in an ongoing way. The following goals are developed in consideration of Erik Erikson's developmental stages and Lawrence Kohlberg's stages of moral development. Use these ideas to develop your own goals.

Infants and Very Young Children Can:

- use their exploratory nature to heighten self-appreciation. (Children cannot recognize and appreciate something different from themselves until they know themselves.)
- experience a trusting environment, so that they have confidence in what happens in the church.
- hear praise for their positive actions. (Recognize that children this age may behave out of fear of punishment. Diverting attention is always preferable to punishment. Praise of positive actions strengthens their self-esteem and helps to set a pattern. Always accompany punishment with love.)
- enjoy parallel play. (Recognize that before age 3, children usually engage in parallel play more than in cooperative games. Provide multiple play objects.)
- have opportunity to play with items such as dolls with various racial traits and dress-up clothes from many cultures. (This gives subtle suggestions of ethnic and cultural differences.)

Children Ages 3–5 Can:

- learn songs, games, and stories from other cultures. (They will not understand the cultural difference, but they can experience a game that they later learn to be the heritage of another culture.)
- learn an occasional word for names and numbers in other languages, as their recognition of these develops. (This age enjoys things that are "different" and will find them exciting.)
- come to know persons from different cultures with positive attitudes. (Invite into the classroom persons who have worked in other countries. Be sure these persons stress the commonality of customs, as well as the differences.)
- use new skills in group activity to develop a sense of belonging and love for one another. (Stress love for one another even while recognizing differentness.)
- develop a growing sense of pride in your church family and a recognition of ways the church helps others.

- realize that persons in our church family come together to study and to worship God, and then go out to serve. (You may help to bring this about by speaking to older preschoolers of the ways individual children have served someone since you last met.)
- grow to recognize and appreciate their own new talents and abilities as they develop. (Express appreciation for the ways the children act as peacemakers, or the times they have discovered ways to help others.)
- learn to look for simple ways to use their abilities to help others. (Speak of our happiness in helping as the reward for our actions.)

Children in Grades 1–3 Can:

- learn to accept responsibility for their own actions and recognize the effect of their actions on others.
- begin to recognize the way Christians around the world tell and show others what God has done. This can happen as their understanding of geography develops. (Introduce the word *witness* through this.)
- enjoy expanded experiences with songs, games, and stories from other cultures.
- recognize that people elsewhere sometimes worship in different ways. (Extended experience in your local patterns and forms of worship acts as a foundation for this.)
- experience additional opportunities to meet people from other countries. (Use pictures and videos that show different ways of doing things. When studying about helpers, look at persons who hold similar positions in other countries. Provide books that include home activities in other cultures.)
- begin to look at situations from different viewpoints.
- grow in management of their personal time and recognize themselves as stewards of their time, learning to use time wisely.
- learn that money is of God's creation and belongs to God. In order to do this, they must learn to recognize money as the result of the way we use our talents, and appreciate the many ways our money functions in the church, including financial necessities to maintain the church.
- expand their understanding of service for others carried out by the church, and develop ways for your class to act in mission.

Children in Grades 4–6 Can:

- grow in understanding of the difference between "justice" and "fair." In justice, everyone has the right to basic needs such as life, food, shelter, education, employment, proper medical care, clean water and air, security of body and emotions, and the opportunity to direct and govern themselves.
- learn to distinguish between independence and interdependence, recognizing that everyone must work together for justice (Matt. 20:1-16).
- develop specific talents and appreciate the ways they may use those talents as stewards.
- begin to see themselves through the eyes of others.
- experience "standing in the moccasins of others."
- develop a more meaningful understanding of facts about our world and relate these to people's lives. (As they develop skills in memory, facts about the world become more meaningful.)
- use newly acquired research and conversational skills to find their own answers about everyday life and celebrations in other cultures.

- develop an appreciation of God's concern for all people and be aware of the ways Christians respond to God's love in mission. (They may be eager to think of ways they can be in mission in their communities, or in other places in the world.)

The following chapters offer many practical suggestions that will help you incorporate stewardship and mission in all aspects of your ministry with children. The suggestions serve various purposes:

- help children recognize similarities and diversity among God's people;
- help children recognize their gifts that enable them to care for God's people;
- encourage children in stewardship and servanthood;
- help children recognize and celebrate other cultures.

Some of the ideas in these chapters came out of the networking that goes on among people in the workshops I teach across the country. Many activities began as seedlings, pruned and shaped by the interchange in those workshops, until they bloomed as healthy hybrids. I thank God for the opportunity to share this harvest of ideas, and I thank the workshop participants for sowing the seeds.

Spontaneous and Planned Experiences

3 The chapel at Candler School of Theology, on the Emory University campus in Atlanta, is painted a soft gray. There are no colorful stained-glass windows, and if you see the room when there is no service, you will find no colorful banners or bright paraments. However, during a service, the room comes alive with color! Color vibrates from the worship center! Faces, hair, clothing—all this color brings the room to life, standing out against the gray background. I understand that the architects designed the chapel in this way to accentuate the color that people bring to the worship experience. I found myself even more conscious of the contrast, once I had been told of the intentional design.

We need to be conscious of experiences that bring color to the ways children may learn to care for God's people. Stewardship and mission can be woven into the fabric of their experiences in the classroom and in worship services. Stewardship and mission can make up the colorful thread that holds the year together. By following your example, and through experiential learning, your children will develop a life-style of caring for God's people.

This chapter lifts up many spontaneous opportunities that we may skip over if we become mundane in our teaching. The latter part of the chapter includes several experiences that you may want to plan for specific times. Remember that learning takes place in many settings in the church. Think carefully about ways classroom experiences can be connected to worship, or expanded in other ways beyond the classroom.

Using Your Regular Curriculum

Be aware of opportunities to teach stewardship and mission as you use your regular curriculum, even when the theme seems to have no emphasis on these subjects. Look for opportunities to intersperse information about other cultures and other parts of the world, and look for opportunities to lift up stewardship. Examples:

- On a study about worship, include information on worship styles that are different from your own. Select translations of familiar hymns in other languages.
- When studying how the Bible came to us across the years, look at various translations in today's languages. Explain that even with a common language such as English, people with different backgrounds arrive at different understandings of what is written in the Bible. Different languages also reach different understandings.
- If studying a text with reference to sheep or shepherds, include shepherds of various cultures today, not just the biblical shepherds.
- When the scripture passage mentions trees or flowers, look at pictures of trees in many countries; talk about our stewardship of God's world.
- When your curriculum speaks of families, include families from other cultures. *National Geographic* is a good resource for such pictures.

- In addition to those included with your current curriculum, locate different illustrations of the same Bible story. Stress how various artists visualized the story. Check your picture file for illustrations that use facial features from different cultures.

Recognize Similarities

At every possible opportunity, recognize and mention similarities among children in your classroom, as well as between your children and people elsewhere in the world. These might include: children everywhere enjoy play; we live in families; we all have sad times and happy times; we need clothing in cold weather (in comparison to animals with fur); we all enjoy music; as babies, we are helpless, and we grow some each year until we become adults. Thank God for these similarities, not only during formal prayers, but at spontaneous opportunities.

Celebrate Differences

When differences are pointed out among the children, acknowledge them and affirm the ways God made each of us different and also special. Point out the different talents we have, and how God depends on each of us to use our talent to accomplish caring in the world.

Suggest that the world would be boring if everyone looked exactly alike and enjoyed the same things. Remember that when each person acts as steward of his or her different talents, God's purpose is fulfilled in the world.

Celebrate Our Heritage

Lift up and celebrate persons and families that can trace their roots to other countries. Recognize them as ties with the people elsewhere in the world for whom we care.

Celebrate Past and Present Christian Leaders

Children look to heroes, but we fail to lift up Christian leaders as heroes. Speak frequently about Christians (both living and dead) whom you admire. Seek out stories about them and learn interesting incidents from their lives that will appeal to children.

Invite into the classroom people who exhibit leadership in caring for others. Ask them to join you for a class period, simply being a part of the class. Help the children see these leaders as adult friends. If they become friends who can recognize the children and call them by name outside the classroom, their dedication to Christ and to others will become an admired trait. Ask ahead of time if the adult visitors are involved in ministries in which the children can participate.

Assign Stewardship Roles in the Classroom

Some classes assign specific "jobs" for "helpers" to do each week. Change your terminology, and use the word *steward*. Ask a child if he or she will be "Steward of the Crayons" this week. The person helping to pass out snacks becomes "Steward of the Snacks/drinks/napkins."

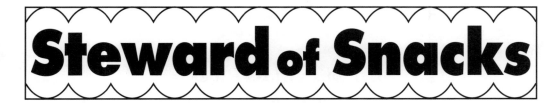

Instead of simply asking children to erase the chalkboard, ask them to be "Stewards for the Chalkboard." (See "Create a Service Towel" in chapter 4.)

Teach Spontaneously in Play Centers

We must recognize that play is the work of young children. They learn through play. Centers in a classroom need adults nearby, aware of the action as it occurs, occasionally interacting with the children. Speak up and affirm students who show caring for each other and caring for "pretend" persons/dolls. Here are some examples:

- When the child pretends that a doll has been hurt, say, "Show me how you can make the doll feel better. How did you help? Have you ever done something to make a real person feel better?"
- When the child "serves" a meal to another in the housekeeping area, say, "Charles, I like the way you show caring for Rachel by serving her the meal."
- When a play car runs into another car, "I wonder how the people in the cars feel. Do you suppose they are hurt? How can the people in the other cars help them?"
- When a child makes a picture or builds a tower of blocks, say, "Your talent in drawing/building is a real gift from God!"
- When caring for an animal or watering plants you might have in the classroom, say, "Thank you for being a steward of God's animal/plant."
- When looking at a nature wonder center, say, "Didn't God create a wonderful world? How can we act as stewards of God's world?"

Care for Others During Snacks

Allow children who are old enough to handle a pitcher to pass it, so that each child can pour the drink into a neighbor's cup, all around the table. Then give thanks, not only for the drink, but for the servers who care for each other.

Use Disputes to Teach Caring

After determining the source of the dispute, ask each child to explain the *other* person's point of view, or how the other person understands what happened. Then ask for two or three solutions, with each child stating how the other person might react to that solution. Together, agree on a common solution. (This gives two opportunities for the child to stand in another person's shoes.)

Search for Answers Together

When answers don't come easily in a classroom, help children feel comfortable while searching for answers. Always acknowledge all answers as legitimate thoughts. You might say something like, "You've really put some thought into that. I appreciate your thoughts. What are some other thoughts on this?"

Our computer world has developed an "instant answer" society. By creating an inquiring atmosphere in the classroom, you will help children feel comfortable with ideas from other cultures.

Establish Class Rules

Help children establish rules that will be carried out in the classroom. To do this, ask the children what actions help them to work together and what actions keep them from working together happily. Ask what rules they might agree on that would keep the class working together happily. Stress positive wording of rules where possible. When the children set their own rules, they will help one another uphold the rules.

Teach Caring Through Choices

I will always appreciate my father's method of driving about town. Each time we traveled, he selected a different route. I learned early on that we could arrive at the same location by traveling different roads.

As adults, we often insist that things should be done "our" way because our experience gives us insight into the best, easiest, or shortest solution. However, when we insist on this, we send signals to children that there is only one way to accomplish things, thereby hampering their appreciation of other people and various ways of living. Give children several options and recognize as legitimate each workable solution to a problem.

Responses to a Hungry, Thirsty, or Cold Student

Be alert to opportunities to make a bridge between the student's feelings and the feelings of other people. Simply stress the feelings of the student, creating concern, but not laying a guilt trip on him or her. This may be done with words such as: "Oh, I'm sorry you are hungry. How does it feel? Does it sort of pull at your stomach? Umm, that must be how a child in _____ might feel when he or she has only one bowl of rice each day." (Or, "It must be how the children in your school feel when they have no breakfast before coming to school.")

Acknowledge Common Needs

Whenever the following needs are mentioned during class time or in individual conversations, remind children that each person has a right for these needs to be fulfilled. Encourage discussion of what it might be like not to have some specific need fulfilled.

Common physical needs	food, shelter, medical care
Common emotional needs	a family environment; to be loved, safe, accepted, not left out
Common intellectual needs	education for a functional life (for children, this includes play)
Common spiritual needs	freedom to worship; opportunity to learn about God

Distinguish Between Needs and Wants

Children learn language use according to what we as adults accept and encourage. Encourage children to distinguish between needs and wants by reminding them to use the term "I want" or "I would like" instead of "I need" in appropriate situations.

Using magazines and catalogs, encourage the children to cut out pictures of items they like and need. Divide sheets of paper down the middle, labeling one side "I need," and the other side "I like." Discuss the children's pictures, and as they paste them on the appropriate side, help them understand which are needs, and which are things we'd like to have. Make a cover and fasten the sheets together with staples or a piece of yarn.

Sharing Time

Consider setting a routine time during your class period (it may be at the beginning of the class, in the middle, or at the end) to invite students to share a care or concern for others.

With older children, encourage conversation about happenings beyond the community, including news in other countries. This time might be closed with a prayer for these concerns.

Learn Words in Other Languages

Where possible, locate people in your own church who speak other languages. Invite them into the classroom, or ask someone to assist you in translating greetings for the children to learn. Throughout the year, use greetings in other languages frequently. If you do not have someone to translate for you, use the greetings listed below.

Filipino Greetings

Mabuhay—Welcome (as being welcomed to a festival or church) (*mah-BOO-high*)
Magandang Umaga—Good morning (*Mah-gahn-dahngoo-mah-gah*)
Magandang Hapon—Good afternoon (*Mah-gahn-dahnghah-pohn*)
Magandang Gabi—Good evening (*Mah-gahn-danggah-bee*)
Kumusta Kayo—How are you? (singular) (*Koo-moo-stah Kigh-oh*)
Kumusta Po—Polite form, such as "How are you, sir or ma'am?" (*Koo-moo-stah Poh*)

(*Church Times*, Grades 1-3 [Nashville: Graded Press, Winter 1989-90])

Russian Greetings (spelled phonetically)

Kristos Vos Kres—Christ is risen.
Voistin Vos Kres—Indeed, he is risen.

(*Teacher in the Church Today* [Nashville: Cokesbury, April 1992], p. 14.)

Learn Names of Plants and Animals

At every opportunity, learn names of plants and animals. Learn something about the life patterns and needs of these also. When we know something by name and become acquainted with its needs we naturally have more interest in caring for it.

Stress Recycling in the Classroom

(See chapter 2 concerning recycling in the classroom.)

Set up the "R Rule."

Reduce

Reuse   These 3 r's bring about **R**esponsibility.

Recycle

Recognize Recycle Symbol

Point out the recycle symbol on items that you use. You may want to have students search for the symbol at home and on a specific day everyone bring any items they have found with the symbol.

Investigate how the church office uses recycled products and saves office papers for recycling. Encourage the use of the symbol on flyers and such when using recycled paper.

Planned Experiences

Stewardship Centers for Children

Set up four centers in your room for children to visit at some time during each session. Make a sign with the following instructions for each center:

Prayer	Presence	Gifts	Service
Write or draw a prayer of thanks or a concern.	Check your name off the attendance list.	Place your offering in the basket or your gift for others in the box.	Draw or write a way you cared for God's people this week.

Make and Break Creation

This experience is appropriate for older elementary children. You will need materials that can be used to make, take apart, and remake something, such as blocks, clay, or pipe cleaners. The experience will be done with a partner.

1. Each person makes an individual "creation." After making the creation, each person tells the partner about the creation.
2. Partners then exchange creations, and each person tears the partner's creation apart.
3. Afterward, come together as a class and discuss:

- How did you feel while you made your creation?
- How did you feel when you told your partner about your creation?
- How did you feel while you tore your partner's creation apart?
- How did you feel when you looked at your own creation after your partner had torn it apart?

4. Each pair works together to build a better creation, using materials from both of their destroyed creations.

Rice for All

Purchase a bag of rice. Check the number of servings in the bag, and calculate how many pews of people in your church one (or two) such bags will feed. Have those people stand during a service, and give each family enough rice to feed four. Ask them to cook and enjoy the rice during the week, then decide on some action they can take to help supply needed food for others around the world. In the bulletin, include information on this experience and additional information on hunger, so that the families can reflect on it at home.

Shopping Trip

Give a group of children a hypothetical family situation, and arrange with a local grocery store for the children to "shop" by going up and down the aisles, making a list of items the family might put on its grocery list. The family might be a single parent with two children (decide on the ages) and only $20.00 to spend for the next two weeks. As you "shop," talk about just what such a family will need, how much each item costs, and how to make the best choices nutritionally.

Experience a Meal

This experience is appropriate for middle and older elementary children. Plan a meal or snack. Set one table with tablecloth, flowers, glasses, pitchers of iced drink, and so on. Leave the other tables plain. Place numbers 1, 2, and 3 on the bottom of paper plates, according the the size of your class: For each 10 persons, give 6 persons a #3 on their plates (representing people in very deprived countries); give 3 persons a #2 (representing people in less-deprived countries); and give one person a #1 (representing people in well-fed countries).

As students arrive, give out the plates, not allowing anyone to see the numbers on bottom. Then announce that they will be served according to the numbers. Ask those with #1 to come first. Exchange their paper plates for good china and give them some of everything prepared (meat, rice or potatoes and another vegetable, salad, dessert, bread, butter, salt/pepper, knife/fork/spoon, and cloth napkins.) They will sit at the table that has been set with tablecloth, flowers, and iced drink.

Ask the students with #2 to come up. They will use the paper plates and paper napkins and are not served with meat, butter, or dessert. They sit at a table with no tablecloth and have no ice in their drink.

Last, serve the students with #3. They receive only very small portions of rice or potato. They have no napkins or silverware, and their only drink is water with no ice.

After eating for a few minutes, announce to the whole class that there is plenty of food left and that group #1 can have all they want. Invite them to come back for more. (NOTE: This allows group #1 to return and take food to those at the other tables if they want. Don't suggest this, but let the students in group #1 arrive at this solution themselves.) Afterwards, discuss how they felt:

- Someone in group #3, did you feel that you were being treated fairly? How did you feel about yourself? About the other groups?
- Someone in group #2, how did you feel toward group #1? Toward group #3?
- Someone in group #1, how did you feel? When did your feelings begin to change?
- How might you have dealt with the situation differently?
- Do you realize that we in North America are a part of group #1? How do you feel about that? What might we do about it?

Partners Serve

Pair children off in twos. The partner with the closest birthday to a selected date becomes the server for the day. The server will:

- Give the partner a back or neck rub.
- Help the partner find a comfortable seat.
- See that partner has all supplies (paper, scissors, etc.) needed for activity during the class.
- See that partner has treats (such as juice) when they are distributed.

- Help partner with any assignment for the day.

At the end of class session, read Matthew 20:26-28 and Galatians 5:13. Ask those who were servers to come together at one place and draw a collage of ways we can serve. Those who were served meet together in another place, and each writes a thank-you note to their servers.

Come together and share the collage, talk about how each felt being served or serving. As you leave, the children who were served give the servers their thank-you notes.

Count Water Taps in Home

All children can visualize water taps in their homes. Younger children will need to tell you where the water taps are, and you can count them. Or you may want to make a mark, or draw a small water tap for each one they mention. After discussion of the many places in their homes where they can get water to drink, tell them that many people don't have good water in their homes, and some don't even have clean water nearby. Sometimes the women and girls must walk several hours each day, carrying water for their family. Older children who understand concepts of large numbers can begin to comprehend when you tell them that 1.2 billion people don't have water that is safe to drink.

Experiencing Handicaps

At times, curriculum will suggest methods of role-playing a handicap. You might decide on one method, and each week allow one child to go through part or all of the class period using the handicap. Do not try this with children under the age of kindergarten, and use simple items only briefly with kindergartners and first-graders. Older children can work with a handicap for an entire class period. You will find that children who have worked with it in previous weeks become more concerned for those going through it currently. Consider using the following methods, or create your own.

- blindfolded (to experience sightlessness)
- both hands wrapped with an elastic bandage, so that the fingers cannot be used (to experience arthritic hands)
- one leg tied up by wrapping a strip of cloth around the ankle, then around the waist, necessitating the use of a crutch (to experience use of only one leg)
- sit in wheelchair the whole class period (to experience needing a wheelchair)
- right arm (for right-handed persons/left for left-handed persons) tied behind back (to experience use of only one arm)
- ear plugs used throughout class period (to experience inability to hear)

Festivals and Celebrations

(Note: See "Festival of Diversity" and other celebrations in chapter 10.)

Giant Map of the World

This is most appropriate for children who have some understanding of maps.

Paint a map of the world in the parking lot or another cement area. On the map, identify the continents. When a class studies a specific area, the children color that area with colored chalk.

OR

Ask a handy carpenter in your church to make stools of map pieces. These can either be square stools, with the map painted on the tops, so that putting the stools together will solve the "map puzzle," or each stool might be in the shape of a continent, and children move the stools about on the floor to place the continents in their proper locations. By using the stools simply as sitting furniture at other times, you help to make the geography of the world a common understanding.

A Weaver Visits the Classroom

Make arrangements for a weaver to bring a loom into the classroom and work, weaving a variety of colors into the fabric. For young children, this will simply become a foundation for later understanding of how people of different characteristics, background, and talents make up God's family. Most elementary, and a few older preschool children, can grasp the abstract connection.

To make an even more meaningful experience, ask children to bring in fabric from old clothing they can no longer wear. This fabric is then woven into the design, creating a colorful masterpiece that represents your class. Also point out that we act as stewards by recycling the old clothing.

You may even consider helping the children dye natural yarn in the classroom and allowing the children to take turns at the loom, making it a representation of their talents, as well as of their lives.

(See "Create a Quilt, Rug, or 'Sit-upon' " in chapter 4.)

Talents to Share

Read or tell the story in I Kings 17:1-16 (the widow and her son who share meal and oil with Elijah) or John 6:1-15 (the boy who shares his loaves and fish). Talk about how these persons shared what they had.

Give each person (teachers included) a piece of paper. Each person writes his or her name at the top of the paper and tapes it to his or her own back. Everyone thinks of a special talent of each of the people, and then moves about the room, writing a talent on each person's paper.

If there are more than six or eight in your class, you might ask them to stand in a circle before they write the talents on one another's backs. Pair the children off (counting 1, 2; 1, 2). The pairs then face each other and take turns writing on each other's back. At a given signal, they face again, and, looking at their partners, repeat some common statement as a group (such as "Shalom" or "God made you great!"). Then they move forward one person and do the same with the next person, until each person has written on all the backs.

Afterward, allow everyone to read their papers in silence, thinking about how their talents might be used for God. You may play quiet music during this time. Discuss the talents in the class, and then have a prayer of thanksgiving for the talents.

Feeding One Another

Prepare a small meal. Pizza is appropriate, because it is a favorite of children. Before the meal, set the tables with places directly across from each other. Provide a twelve-inch piece of doweling and three strips of fabric (one long and two shorter) for each child.

As the children arrive, tell them that this is an experiment, and in order for them to take part in the experiment, they must fasten a piece of doweling to the inside of one elbow by tying it with the two shorter pieces of fabric. This will keep the elbow straight. The other arm is tied to the child's side with the longer piece of fabric. Then tell them to enjoy their meal. As they work with their condition, one of them may suggest that they feed each other across the table. If this does not materialize, ask them to discuss their common problem together and arrive at a solution.

After the meal, ask them how they felt when they realized that they could not eat the pizza with a straight arm. Talk about how they solved the problem and were able to enjoy the meal by cooperation.

Meet a Tree

I grew up in Florida among the spreading live oak trees. For many years, while my husband managed districts of National Grasslands, our family lived in the prairies of the Dakotas. I grew to appreciate the subtle beauty of that country, though I did miss the massive trees of my childhood. On one occasion when we were traveling in a forested area, I enjoyed the trees so much that I actually wanted to stop the car and hug a tree! Since then, I often allow myself to "drink in" their beauty through my eyes. It's as if I can't get enough of looking at trees!

Illustrated by Tom Armstrong

For this experience, you will need to locate a place with several trees. Here, the children do two things. First, they walk up to a tree, close their eyes, and spend some time feeling the tree trunk. (You may want to provide blindfolds for this part.) Then they sit on the ground, far enough back from the tree to see all parts of it, and make mental notes of everything they observe about the tree. Then they come together as a group and discuss these questions:

- Had you ever hugged a tree before? How did it feel to hug a tree?
- What was the texture of the tree? What did it remind you of?
- What did you find out about the tree that you didn't know before?
- What benefits do we get from trees? (Besides the obvious, be sure to include an esthetic value and an appreciation for God's world.)
- What can we do, as stewards of trees?

Stewardship Cookies

Use the following recipe for fortune cookies, but instead of inserting fortune papers in the cookies, insert papers that state ways we can practice our stewardship. The papers need to be $\frac{1}{2} \times 3$ inches.

Ingredients:

2 large egg whites	1 cup flour
pinch of salt	1 teaspoon instant tea powder
$\frac{2}{3}$ cup sugar	2 tablespoons water
$\frac{1}{4}$ teaspoon vanilla	6 tablespoons margarine, melted

Method:

Mix egg whites with salt and sugar. Stir in, in this order: vanilla, flour, tea, water, and margarine. Mix well and chill thoroughly. Place on greased cookie sheet in small amounts, flattening into 3-inch circles. Bake at 350° for 3 to 5 minutes, or until edges turn brown. Quickly remove cookies from pan, place folded paper in center, bring edges up, and pinch together before cookie hardens. Cool. Encourage each child to share a cookie with someone outside the class and talk about the message in the cookie. Have everyone report back the next week.

Sharing Soup

You may be familiar with the story of *Stone Soup* by Marcia Brown, in which travelers arrive at a town hungry, but no one offers to share any food with them. The travelers offer to make a delicious soup for the village, using a special stone they had brought with them. They prepare the fire and pot and begin boiling the stone, talking about how good the soup will be. In their conversation, they comment that it would be even better if they only had a carrot (or other vegetable) to go into it, and miraculously, someone in the village discovers the vegetable and shares it. (Some versions of this story emphasize the trickery of obtaining the meal, but Brown's version stresses the way sharing results in food for all.) Your class can make the sharing experience from this story come alive for the whole congregation.

To make this experience churchwide, your class needs to plan ahead, inviting everyone in the congregation to join you for a noonday meal of soup on a specific Sunday. On that day, all those who participate bring a vegetable to their Sunday school class, cleaned but not cut up. Your class spends the class period chopping the vegetables to be put into the soup. (If desired, use a soup bone and begin cooking it earlier in the morning to have a good stock.) The soup cooks during the worship hour, and after worship, families feast on the soup and share the story of *Stone Soup.*

To enhance the meal, your class may also want to purchase or bake bread. Frozen loaves work well here, or you may want to have a bread-baking day on Saturday.

Have a Fix-up Day

Set a specific class time for everyone to bring a toy that needs repair. Ask the children to make certain it is repairable. Collect the toys and arrange for a future session, when adults, preferably parents, can come to help with the repairs. This will help to establish such a pattern at home. Work together repairing the toys, so that they may be used again instead of purchasing new ones.

Create a "Forest" of Newspapers

Ask children to bring in old newspapers (or raid your church recycle bin). To create a "forest," stack newspapers around the room in four-foot-high piles. For each four-foot stack, one large tree had to be cut. After creating the stacks, count the number of trees cut down in order to produce the newspapers you brought into class. Return the papers to the recycle bin when you are finished. To make this result more visible, you may want to conduct the experiment in a courtyard, foyer, or fellowship hall, and use recycled green construction paper to make leaves for the newspaper "trees." Invite the congregation to visit your "forest."

Displays from Other Countries

Prepare a multicultural display of a specific item. Invite the whole congregation to contribute to and enjoy the display, but involve the children in its planning, preparing, and advertising. The display might be a collection of: dolls, stamps, bells, crosses, nativity scenes, ethnic costumes, or Bibles in different languages.

Mission Visits During Vacations

Make a missions map or a list of mission projects for families to use when planning their vacations. Contact your church national committee on missions, for listings of missions your church supports.

Conference Call to a Missionary

Set up a conference call for your class, using a speaker phone. Make all the arrangements in advance and have a photo of the missionary available. Decide on specific questions to ask before making the call. Ask that the missionary be remembered in prayer during the next worship service, arranging this with the pastor or worship leader ahead of time.

Greetings in Several Languages During Congregational Worship

During several sessions prior to Pentecost, or prior to World Communion Sunday, each Sunday school class teaches the students a greeting in a different language. At a specific time during the worship service, invite everyone to greet one another in the language they learned. In the bulletin, list the classes with the words they learned. Those who were not in a class may select one of those words or greet someone in English. During the service, read Acts 2:1-13, then mention how quickly the writer of Acts moves from talking about God's gift of the Holy Spirit to the missionary actions of the disciples.

Celebrate Epiphany and Pentecost

The season of Epiphany emphasizes the life and teachings of Jesus, particularly his acts of caring and his stories about our responsibility to care for others. Because of the celebration of the visit of the wise men (Matt. 2:1-12) during this season, we emphasize increasing global awareness. You may find that your curriculum also carries this theme.

Our Christian celebration of Pentecost (Acts 2:1-13) stems from the event after Christ's death, when the Holy Spirit came upon his followers. There was a large gathering in Jerusalem—people had come from many countries to worship together in the Temple. Consequently, many different languages were spoken. When the followers of Christ were gathered and the Holy Spirit came, they understood one another's different languages. This makes Pentecost the perfect season for stressing our global understanding and appreciation of others.

Introduce preschool children to these seasons and the basic themes. Older children can understand *why* we emphasize the themes during these specific seasons. It is important, however, that we expand our caring for others beyond this season.

Communion Experiences

Enhance your communion services and increase the congregation's global awareness at the same time. Here are some ideas you and your class might suggest that the worship committee include in your congregational service. As you study other countries, you may come up with other ideas.

- To display the elements on the communion table, use plates and large goblets from various countries.
- Ask families representative of various cultures to bake a bread of their heritage for use in communion.
- For each communion celebration, have a person dressed in a different ethnic costume present the elements.
- Study a different country before each communion service, then design and make a tablecloth or bread cover representing that country.
- Make a stole for the pastor. Prior to each communion service, classes study about a particular country and add a symbol from that country to the pastor's stole.
- Be sure your church observes Worldwide Communion (first Sunday in October), stressing that on this particular Sunday, Christians all over the world celebrate the sacrament together.
- For Worldwide Communion, bake breads from countries that receive your mission money.

Information about the countries highlighted each Sunday, as well as the donors and participants, should be included in the bulletin.

Celebrations from Other Cultures

Learn and experience the way seasons are observed in other countries. Books in your local library should be helpful in finding such information. With preschool and early elementary children, simply enjoy the custom, mentioning that this is the way children in _____ country celebrate this particular season. Involve older children in the selection of specific countries or ethnic backgrounds, and the research of customs and games of the season.

Label Church Entrance

Make a sign for your church door: "Servant Entrance."

Adopt Grandparents

Children today have little opportunity to get to know senior adults. In our mobile society, grandparents often live half-way across the country and often see their grandchildren for only a few days each year.

Arrange for families to adopt older adults as grandparents. Families might enjoy doing some of these with adopted grandparents:

- Exchange cards, gifts, and favors.
- Attend worship services together.
- Attend family-night dinners together.
- Make a scrapbook of family activities and discuss these with the adopted grandparents.
- Listen together to tunes that were hits during the adopted grandparents' youth. (Check your local library.)
- Look at photos of the grandparents as teens. Talk about what they did. Compare the feelings they had with the feelings children have today. Stress the similarities.
- Play games and encourage conversation about memories, people, events, thoughts, hopes, and dreams.

Celebrate God's World!

Invite everyone in church to bring from home a potted plant, a vase of flowers or weeds, or the branch of a tree, on an appointed Sunday. Use these to decorate the front of the sanctuary. Use scripture and songs that point out the beauty of God's creation and our responsibility as stewards.

Teaching Through Art and Craft Activities

4 Children learn through experience, and every child learns differently. Some will enjoy creating an art or craft item, some will prefer using words, and others learn best through drama or active games. Provide a variety of ways for children to learn to care for God's people. Encourage all the children to participate in all activities, and place your emphasis on creating, instead of on the finished product.

Art and craft activities not only give children experience, but each time they see or use the object they made, they renew the feelings experienced during their learning. Remember, we teach Christian education, not art. The activity acts as a method to reach our goal—teaching children to care for God's people. Because of our product-oriented society, children learn to focus on their finished creation, rather than appreciating the creative process. As the children work, offer positive comments. You may simply say, "Tell me something about your picture. How did you feel as you were drawing it?" Encourage them to talk about their feelings, about the piece, and about the process.

As you display their creations in the classroom or elsewhere in the church, talk about how the art or craft item helps you think about caring for God's people, about the ways God created us different, or about our responsibility as stewards. Develop pride in their ability to convey the theme, rather than their ability to produce an artistic piece.

From time to time, you will want to display some of their art in the classroom. Keep it current, replacing it with new creations. When items do go home, encourage the children to talk with their families about what they learned. Help them recognize that they can use their creations to share their learning with others.

When selecting any of the suggested activities in this chapter, consider the abilities of your children. Have they developed eye-hand coordination? How do they handle scissors, glue, or pencils? Although it is important to help children experience satisfaction in their work, rather than frustration, our goal centers around the learning, not the finished product.

As you plan to use a specific activity, make certain that you first experiment with it yourself. This gives you a clear understanding of how the activity should be carried out. Although each activity in this chapter lists specific supplies, your experiment will enable you to better help the students, and also will produce an example for the students to see. If your talents in art are like mine, the children will realize that you do not expect their products to be perfect!

In choosing specific activities for this book, I cautiously avoided food items, unless such an item is to be eaten later. This is particularly important as we teach children about stewardship and caring for God's people. When we tell children, on one hand, about people who starve because they have no food, and then turn around and prepare a craft or art object that uses food, we send a mixed message. So consider using small rocks, broken shells, twigs, bits of paper, old crayon shavings, broken eggshells, and colored sand, rather than beans, macaroni, or rice in those projects.

Wherever possible, help the children think of throwaway items that can be recycled in their projects. Encourage adults in your church to save such items, and arrange a place in your supply room to store them. You might advertise in your church newsletter for a volunteer to organize and maintain such a room. Consider using the following wording in order to locate a person with this talent:

> Do you enjoy seeing things in their proper place? Does it satisfy you to bring order out of chaos? Then organization is one of your gifts from God. Consider a ministry of coordinating our supply room by calling _____.

As you plan to use a specific activity, recognize it as a learning tool. Recognize that you and the children are co-creators with God.

Banners

Create banners with titles: "We are all servants of the Lord." or "Alike but different, God created us all." Banners may be made from felt, recycled bed sheets, or another fabric. Decorate them with fabric crayons, colored markers, or tempera paints.

Handprint/Footprint Banner

Consider making a banner with the prints of many hands (or feet) by mixing tempera paints in dishpans, adding a small amount of liquid detergent for easy cleanup. Dip hands (or feet) into the paint and then place them (or walk) across the sheet or other fabric.

Involve the whole church by setting the banner-making materials in a common area and inviting everyone to participate with the children. Ask your pastor or worship leader if the banner can be used in worship some Sunday.

Materials Needed: Fabric or bed sheet of light, solid color; fabric crayons and iron, or colored markers, or tempera paint; dishpans, water, towels.

Banners of Names

Using the first letters of their names, children can create banners that state ways they can care for God's people.

> **L** augh with someone who is lonely.
> **A** ddress newsletters for the church.
> **U** ndo a young child's winter coat.
> **R** emove leaves from an older person's yard.
> **A** rrange to visit a nursing home.

Materials Needed: Paper or fabric; markers or crayons.

Bird Feeder

Several designs may be used for bird feeders. The simplest is made by cutting a large hole in one side of a gallon plastic milk container, about one inch from the bottom. Be sure the cap is secure on the container. For hanging, make small holes on either side of the neck of the bottle, just below the cap, and thread a string or wire through the holes. Cover the bottom with seed and hang the bird feeder in the yard.

You may want to make a bird feeder by attaching a wire to a large pine cone for hanging. Then spread peanut butter on the pine cone and roll it in birdseed.

Materials Needed: Gallon plastic milk container, or pine cone and peanut butter; birdseed; wire or string; scissors.

Birdnest Supermarket

Use mesh bags from onions or other vegetables. Fill the bags with string, hair from a hairbrush, small bits of fabric or cotton, etc. Hang from a porch or in a tree. Sprinkle birdseed on the ground nearby to attract birds.

Materials Needed: Mesh bags; pieces of string, hair, cotton, bits of fabric, etc.; birdseed (optional).

Bubble Painting

Fill a small bowl about half full of thin tempera paint. Add about one teaspoon of dish detergent. Using a straw, blow in the bowl of tempera paint to make bubbles. Then place a paper over the bowl and the bubbles. As the bubbles pop, they will leave a unique design on the paper. Notice that each bubble is different, and each design is different. Recognize that people also are different.

Materials Needed: Small bowl; thin tempera paint; dish detergent; straws; sheets of paper.

Bumper Stickers or Badges

For your badges or bumper stickers, consider using statements such as these:

I (recycle symbol) Recycle.

I (heart) the world.

I (heart) all people.

Materials Needed: Light-colored adhesive paper; marking pens (permanent markers work best).

Communion Trays or Clay Pots

Native Americans used clay pots for cooking and serving. To make a pot, on waxed paper, first roll a small piece of clay into a thin rope. Turn a bowl upside down and spread baby oil on the outside. Place one end of the clay rope at the center of the overturned bowl, then wind the rope around the bowl, pressing each ring close to the previous ring as you go. Keep the clay wet by dipping your fingers in water as you work. Continue to roll ropes of clay and press them around the bowl. Connect each new rope by pressing one end of it against the end of the previous one.

When the bowl is covered, you may let it dry, leaving the coiled design. Or you may press the coils flat while they are still wet, smoothing the ridges and seams with wet hands. The smoothed sides may be decorated with designs by using toothpicks or other small instruments. Be careful not to weaken the pot by pressing the design too deep. The artist's name may be imprinted on the bottom of the pot.

When the clay is completely dry, turn it right side up and carefully lift the bowl from the dried clay.

These could be used for a communion celebrated with the whole church family. The origin and design of these communion trays should be noted in the bulletin. (NOTE: These bowls should be lined with a napkin and used only for bread. There may be a health risk if used for juice or wine.)

Materials Needed: Clay that will dry without a kiln; bowl of desired size; water; toothpicks.

Decomposing Timeline

Using a large paper, make and illustrate a graph, using the following information. You may prefer to make this on a bulletin board and fasten the actual objects to the graph.

Materials Needed: Large paper or bulletin board; markers or crayons.

Long Time Litter

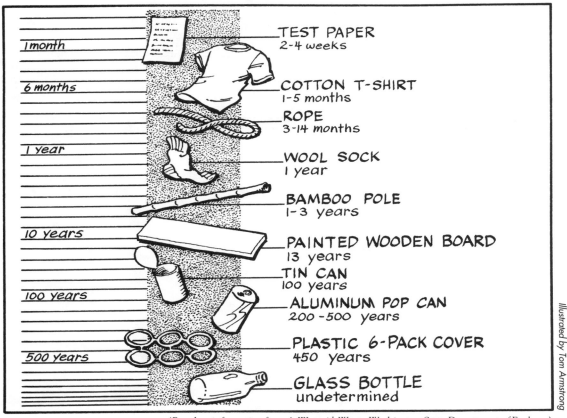

1 month	TEST PAPER 2-4 weeks
6 months	COTTON T-SHIRT 1-5 months
	ROPE 3-14 months
1 year	WOOL SOCK 1 year
	BAMBOO POLE 1-3 years
10 years	PAINTED WOODEN BOARD 13 years
	TIN CAN 100 years
100 years	ALUMINUM POP CAN 200-500 years
	PLASTIC 6-PACK COVER 450 years
500 years	GLASS BOTTLE undetermined

Illustrated by Tom Armstrong

(Based on information from *A-Way with Waste*, Washington State Department of Ecology.)

Devotional Book

Reproduce the form below. Ask the children to illustrate and fill in these pages for a booklet to be given to every church family. This might be prepared for the Week of Christian Unity, or for Lent. Consider using the following verses: Psalm 34:13-14; Matthew 5:43-44; II Corinthians 13:11; Ephesians 4:1-6; I Thessalonians 5:15; I Peter 3:8-9.

Materials Needed: Copies of page 38; crayons or markers; stapler or yarn for assembling book.

DEVOTIONAL

Date:

Bible verse: _____

_____

_____

When Christians care about one another, they _____

_____

_____

_____

(Draw illustration here.)

Pray: **Dear God,** _____

_____

_____ **Amen.**

My name _____ Age _____

Group Picture

Draw a picture as a group, each person adding a part. Before beginning, the group discusses the theme and just what might be included. The group could plan ahead of time who will add what part to the picture, or could allow people to decide what to add when it is their turn.

As an example, the picture might illustrate a mission project, in which (1) a man saws a board, (2) a woman hammers nails, and (3) a child paints (4) a wall of a house, while (5) the owner (an older person) looks on with pride.

Materials Needed: Large paper; crayons, markers, or paints.

Illustrate Ways to Recycle Missiles

Read Micah 4:3 and Matthew 5:9. Then ask the children to draw pictures of ways that missiles might be recycled into something that can be used for peace.

Materials Needed: Paper; crayons.

Illustrate World Resources Distribution

Ask each child to divide a paper plate into three equal sections. In two-thirds of the plate, ask the children to draw six faces and put their name on one of those faces. Now ask them to draw 94 faces in the other one-third of the plate. Explain that the six faces represent the 6 percent of the world population that has two-thirds of the world resources, and the 94 faces represent the 94 percent of the world population that has one-third of the resources. Discuss how your church or denomination is working to provide resources to those who have too few.

Materials Needed: Paper plates; pencils or crayons.

Junk Sculpture, or a Fuddlejig

Ask children to bring discarded items from home. Make two junk sculptures, one from recycleable items and one from nonrecycleable items. Put a smile on the recycleable sculpture and a frown on the other.

Or you may want to read Stanford Summers' book, *Wacky and His Fuddlejig* (New York: Red Ink Productions, 1980), a story about a factory worker who substitutes a fuddlejig for war toys. The fuddlejig is a fun toy made from discarded items. After reading the story, invite each child to make a fuddlejig, using discarded items.

Material Needed: Discarded items; glue or glue gun.

Light-switch Covers

Use plain-colored adhesive paper, cut to the size of electrical switch covers. Use permanent markers or paints to decorate the covers, including a statement such as, "God's stewards turn off lights." Remove the backing and place on switch covers at church and at home.

Materials Needed: Adhesive paper; markers or paints.

Litter Bags

Decorate litter bags for the family, or to be distributed to the whole church. These may be small plastic or brown paper bags, or made from heavy paper:

1. Fold and glue two inches of the top edge forward.
2. Fold bottom edge up to barely cover glued section. Glue or tape this along left and right edges.
3. To hang, punch two holes, side by side, in the top two inches, and run yarn through.
4. Decorate.

Materials Needed: Plastic or brown paper bags, or heavy paper; markers; glue; tape; hole punch; yarn; markers or crayons.

Mola Designs

Mola designs come from the Cuna people of San Blas Islands, on the eastern coast of Panama. The women embroider overlays of bright cloth on their clothing.

To make a design characteristic of a mola, use a simple drawing, such as the dove below. Slightly enlarge the drawing twice, as indicated, to create three patterns of different sizes. Cut each size from different colors of construction paper and glue them together, the largest on the bottom and the smallest on top, so that the edges of the previous papers show all around the design. Place the finished design on white paper and frame with a one-inch frame of construction paper.

Materials Needed: Construction paper; scissors; glue.

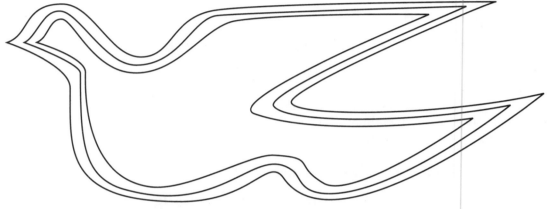

Mountain of Great Commission

Place a mural of a mountain on a wall or bulletin board. On the mural, print the words from Matthew 28:19-20. Add to the display maps and pictures of the mission activities your church sponsors and takes part in. Renew the display regularly.

Materials Needed: Large paper or newsprint; maps and pictures of mission activities; markers or paints.

Mural of Church Stewardship

Make a mural that depicts the ways your money helps your particular congregation carry on Christ's ministry: salaries, cleaning supplies and equipment, office supplies and equipment, electricity, water, phone, lawn-care equipment, gas for trips, vans to pick up the elderly, musical instruments, sheet music, curriculum, toys, Bibles, library books, hymnals, etc.

For young children, label the areas ahead of time, and ask the children to illustrate various areas with pictures. Older children can interview leaders of the church and decide on which areas to label and illustrate.

Talk about how supporting the local church helps outreach to members and other persons in the community, and also trains the people (including the children) in the ways they can help God's people.

Materials Needed: Large paper; crayons or markers.

Newspaper Logs

Using a length of old broomstick, start tightly rolling newspaper around it, one section after another. Before reaching the end of each piece, tuck another section in a few inches. When the log is two inches thick, slip out the broomstick and tie the bundle with light wire. These logs can be soaked, by adults only, in kerosene (never gasoline), in a tray made from a sheet of heavy-duty aluminum foil. Once the log has soaked up the fluid, wrap enough newspaper around each cord to make a five-inch thick log and tie it with light wire. Three logs will burn all evening in a fireplace.

Materials Needed: Newspapers; broomstick; light wire; kerosene; heavy-duty aluminum foil.

Peace Pyramid

Draw, or build with boxes, a pyramid. Illustrate and label three parts of the pyramid:
Materials Needed: Paper or boxes; markers.

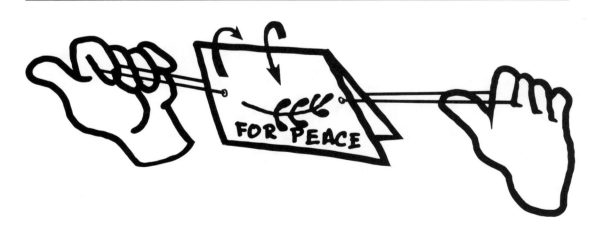

Peace Spinner

Fold a sheet of construction paper in half . Then unfold it, and below the center fold line, write "For Peace." Above these words, draw an olive branch (see picture).

Above the center fold line, write "Let's Work." Below these words, draw a dove in flight.

Refold the paper, with the words on the outside, and punch a hole in the center of both short sides (see picture). Pull a double length of yarn through each set of holes on the short sides of the folded paper.

Hold one of the doubled lengths of yarn in each hand (see picture). Twist with your thumb and finger to make the spinner spin, and watch the dove catch the olive branch.

Materials Needed: Construction paper; yarn; markers or crayons; hole punch.

(*Invitation: Bible Studies for Elementary B* [Nashville: Graded Press, Fall 1991], p. 12)

Poster for Love

Ask children to create posters illustrating caring for God's people. They might be titled "God made the world; I love the world," or "God made people; I love people." Hang the posters where they may be viewed by the whole church, or in strategic places around the community.

Materials Needed: Poster board or large paper; markers or crayons.

Poster of Steward

Make a large poster similar to the drawing below. Ask the children to think of ways the different parts of their body can care for God's people, and write those ways beside the appropriate body parts. Some of their ideas might include:

- Eat an inexpensive meal and send extra money to others who need food.
- Listen for opportunities to help others.
- Tell others about people who are hungry.
- Make bread or cookies to share with someone.
- Sing about the ways God wants us to love others.
- Prepare a box for the whole church to use for collecting food, and see that it is distributed.
- Participate in a walk-a-thon to raise money for others.
- Fold newsletters for the church.
- Use cloth towels and napkins instead of paper.
- Compost natural kitchen waste.
- Pick up and recycle litter.
- Turn off water while brushing teeth.
- Turn out lights when not in use.
- Cut up plastic six-pack rings to protect animals.

Prayer Wheel

Divide a paper plate into seven parts. List a mission project on each of the seven parts. Make a pointer from a strip of paper, and fasten it to the center of the plate with a metal brad. This allows the pointer to be moved each day to a different mission project for which to pray.

Materials Needed: Paper plates; strips of paper; metal brads.

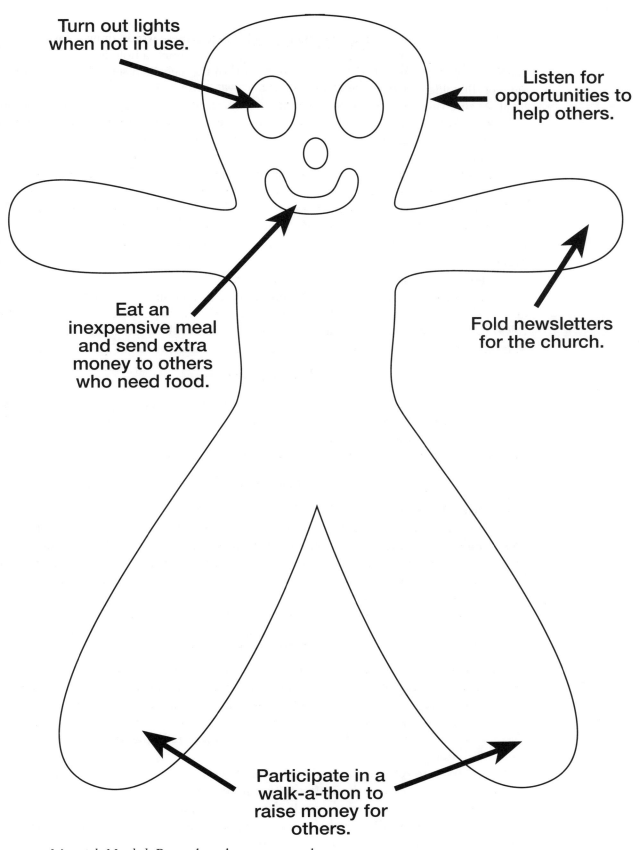

Turn out lights when not in use.

Listen for opportunities to help others.

Eat an inexpensive meal and send extra money to others who need food.

Fold newsletters for the church.

Participate in a walk-a-thon to raise money for others.

Materials Needed: Poster board or paper; markers.

Quilt, Rug, or "Sit-upon"

Ask children to bring from home old items of clothing that may be cut up. Older children can cut these into squares; younger children may watch you cut them. Lay out the squares to make a design. If possible, bring a sewing machine into the classroom to stitch the fabric together, asking each child to bring his or her square to you when it is needed. Use the quilt as a covering for your worship center, as a wall hanging, or as a mat for outdoor events or storytelling.

The same procedure can be used for making a rug—tear the old clothing into strips, and either braid the rug or make a punch rug, using a canvas.

To make sit-upons, use either squares or strips from the old clothing. Have the children exchange their pieces of fabric, so that each person has at least one piece from every member of the class. Then either piece the squares into individual small quilts, or make small, individual rugs for sit-upons.

For young children, this experience will simply become a foundation for their later understanding that people of different characteristics, background, and talents make up God's family. Most elementary, and a few older preschool children can grasp the abstract connection. (NOTE: "See A Weaver Visits the Classroom" in chapter 3.)

Materials Needed: Old items of clothing; scissors; thread and needles or sewing machine.

Talent Search

Using magazines, ask each child to search for three pictures of things he or she does well, and mount them on construction paper. Add the child's name to the paper, and ask each child to tell about the pictures. These may be used for name tags.

Materials Needed: Construction paper; magazines; scissors; glue.

Totem Pole

A Native American totem pole told the story of a tribal nation. Create a totem pole for your class, or have each child create a totem pole for his or her family. Decorate with illustrations about things liked by different persons in the class or family, or about activities the class or family enjoys. Small totems may be made with empty paper-towel rolls; larger ones, by rolling a poster board into a large "pole." For a more permanent one, a round fence post could be painted white.

Materials Needed: Paper-towel rolls, poster board, or round fence post; paints or crayons.

Towels of Service

On a small towel, using fabric paints or permanent markers, illustrate scriptures about serving or ways that people serve. These might be individual towels, or one might be made for the classroom. Use John 13:1-17 to explain the symbol of a towel.

For individual towels, each week, an illustration of one way each person served another person that week could be added. At the end of a designated time, the children could take their towels home.

If a classroom towel is made, use it as a symbol of service, to be worn by anyone acting as God's steward or as a server during a specific class period (such as the person responsible for putting away supplies or serving a snack). You may want to make a towel for each regularly assigned responsibility, using symbols for that responsibility. Keep a belt in the classroom, so that when the towel is worn, it may be looped over the belt.

Scriptures that might be used: Matthew 20:25-28; Matthew 25:14-21; Luke 16:13; John 12:23-26; I Corinthians 12:4-6; I Peter 5:2-4.

Materials Needed: Small towel(s), or fabric hemmed on sides and frayed on edges; fabric paints or permanent markers.

T-shirts

Talk about how we can share our ideas with other people. A T-shirt is one way to tell others what we think. Using white or light-colored T-shirts, children can create their own designs to express the way Christians care for others. Spend time helping the children decide on their own messages before you begin the project.

Materials Needed: White or light-colored T-shirts; permanent markers, fabric paint, or fabric crayons and iron.

World Map

Post a large world map in the center of a bulletin board. Around the edges, post pictures, information, and letters from the various missions your church supports. Use colored yarn to connect the items posted to the mission location on the map. Use gold cord to connect your city with the different mission locations. (Be certain to include missions served through your donations to your national church organization.)

Materials Needed: Large world map; letters, pictures, and information on missions; yarn of different colors; gold cord.

World of Friends

Using different colors of tempera paint, children dip their hands into the paint and place the prints across a large wall map of the world, each hand touching the next.

Materials Needed: Large world map; tempera paint of different colors (with a few drops of dish detergent); dishpan; water and towels.

Worship Paraments

Before each communion celebration, research and study a different country served in mission by the church. Make a set of stoles, or scarfs for the pulpit and communion table, or communion napkins to represent that country. You may also want to bake some bread representative of that country to be used for that communion. Arrange for a notice to be placed in the bulletin about the mission emphasis, naming the class that made the paraments and/or baked the bread.

A white sheet with some acrylic content may be used to make the communion table covering. Fabric crayons give a watercolor effect to designs, which may be made on individual sheets of paper and ironed onto the fabric. There must be some acrylic content in the fabric in order for it to absorb fabric crayons.

Materials Needed: Sheet and/or fabric; fabric crayons, paint, or permanent markers; iron.

Wreath of Hands

Trace all the children's hands on construction paper and cut these out. Mount a picture of a mission project on a round piece of cardboard and glue all the cut-out hands around the picture, with the fingers pointing out, making a wreath. Print the verse from Isaiah 35:3 below the picture or on one of the hands.

Materials Needed: Construction paper; cardboard; scissors; glue; mission picture.

Chain of People

Using white paper, cut out "gingerbread-type" people, with arms reaching out. Ask the children to color and decorate each one in a different manner. Encourage them to use different skin tone and hair colors. Tape the people together so that they seem to be holding hands. Look at the different ways they are decorated, and talk about the ways all people are different, and each one is loved by God.

Materials Needed: White paper; scissors and tape; crayons.

Creation Box, or Nature Sculpture

Either take a field trip to find items from nature, or ask the children to bring items from their own yards. Working in teams, divide a shallow box with cardboard strips and glue nature items in the box. Select a Bible verse about creation and glue this in the box also. (NOTE: See chapter 3 concerning using food for craft activity.)

Materials Needed: Items from nature; glue or glue gun; shirt boxes or other shallow boxes; cardboard strips; scissors.

Teaching Through Drama, Storytelling, and Reflection

Jesus used teaching methods that today's education circles often call "new." Three of those methods are drama, storytelling, and reflection. We easily recognize the parables as a form of storytelling. Sometimes he used this method with individuals or an intimate group, and sometimes he told stories to a large listening audience. And he didn't always give the listeners a "moral" with his story. In fact, he told them, "He who has ears, let him hear."

Jesus encouraged reflection on his stories and on the other thoughts he brought before the people. His suggestion for private prayer in chapter 6 of Matthew suggests reflection. Jesus also practiced reflection himself. We find reference to this in Matthew 14:22-23; Matthew 26:36-43; Mark 1:35; Mark 14:32-39; Luke 5:15-16; and Luke 6:12-16.

As far as the method of drama, I don't recall a large pageant production in the Gospels, and Jesus never organized a children's playhouse theater. But you can't get much more dramatic than walking on water, washing feet, and a symbolic meal. The drama he created was personal, with learner involvement.

Teaching Through Drama

Jesus taught in an experiential way, and children learn best through experience. As I write this, I am learning about handicapping conditions in a most dramatic and experiential way. I broke my leg and must use crutches. I have found new and innovative ways to take a shower and to move things from place to place, and I have learned to rely on others when I cannot handle an activity. Now I have more appreciation for the availability of handicap parking and easy access to buildings and restrooms.

We must remember that the best use of drama in Christian education will benefit the participant rather than the spectator. Look for opportunities to enable children to feel as if they are someone else, to "walk in another's moccasins."

Clowning

Clowning offers children an ideal opportunity to express feelings that they might not ordinarily feel comfortable revealing. Use it to help children experience how persons may feel before and after God's people act in caring ways toward them.

You don't even need to use costumes or face makeup in the classroom. To ease a group into clowning, ask everyone to act as a clown would act. Remind them that clowns express their feelings through their facial expressions and actions, rather than with words:

1. A happy feeling, be playful and bouncy.
2. An unhappy feeling, with a sad face and droopy walk, perhaps like a wilting flower.
3. Unsure of self, fall down and trip over things. (See precaution below.)

With older children, you may want to identify these three basic types of clowning as white-face, sad-face, and Auguste clown. With all ages, simply state that we can use some of these actions in different ways to express our feelings.

A *word of precaution:* Suggest using the third type of clowning only if it applies directly to your situation. This can be taken as a way to poke fun at the disadvantaged. I would suggest that the class usually work with the first two methods. In all cases, be sure that the negative feelings (droopy, unhappy, clumsy) be followed by positive feelings (happy, playful, bouncy), after God's caring people have acted.

Creative Movement

Most young children freely express themselves through movement. Just watch a two-year-old in the midst of a temper tantrum! Or watch a child twirl around and around just for the pure joy of expression. We must give them permission to use body movements to express their feelings as long as it is not harmful to themselves or others.

Creative movement begins with freeing ourselves to move. Before any experiment with creative movement, spend some time relaxing the body and expressing movement freely. Relaxation can be accomplished with simple games or exercises, such as the following:

1. Act like a boat floating in water, or a kite, bobbing in the wind.
2. Act like a kitten asleep on a rug, who begins to wake and stretch.
3. Walk in different ways—jerky, smooth, stiff, floppy, light-footed, heavy-footed.
4. Sitting on a chair or on the floor, use the top part of your body as if it were a hammer.
5. Act like a flower, slowly opening its petals.

(Adapted from Delia Halverson, *New Ways to Tell the Old, Old Story* [Nashville: Abingdon Press, 1992], p. 36.)

After children feel comfortable with movement, ask them to use their bodies to show how they feel about certain situations. Or tell a story, and at specific times during the story, ask them to use movement to dramatize it.

Older children can express more abstract forms. After working with movement for awhile, they can develop specific motions to accompany hymns or readings. These may be used in congregational worship to help convey the message of caring for God's people. Arrange for them to use motions while the congregation sings a hymn. The following motions may help them begin:

Words	Actions
peace/love flowing from us	*arms outstretched*
love	*hands to heart*
joy	*clap hands or rapid jmotion of hands upward*
giving	*move hands from self to others*
repent/resist evil	*pushing hands down to side and back*
captive	*wrists crossed and lowered*
freed	*hands pulled apart and up*

Echo Pantomime

If you have never used echo pantomime with your class, explain that you will tell a story or say short sentences that include some action, and after each sentence, they will repeat (echo) the sentence and action together. Older children can help create echo pantomimes themselves.

God's People Care

Words	Actions
God's people care in many ways.	*Spread out arms and smile.*
Sometimes we help someone who is ill.	*Rub left arm or knee with right hand.*
Sometimes we cook a meal.	*Make bowl with left hand; stir with right.*
We like to help little children.	*Pet someone small.*
Or listen to someone who is sad.	*Cup hand behind ear.*
Sometimes we write a letter.	*"Write" in hand.*
Or sing a song of joy.	*Cup hands around mouth as if singing.*
Sometimes we hammer nails.	*Pretend to hammer.*
Or even paint a house.	*Use imaginary paint brush.*
You and I are all God's people.	*Point to someone else and then self.*
God's people care in many ways.	*Spread out arms and smile.*

Foot Washing

In the North American culture, we cannot appreciate foot washing because we seldom walk barefoot or with sandals on dusty roads. In fact, we seldom walk enough to cause our feet discomfort!

With young children, make use of opportunities when their feet, hands, or face are dirty. As you wash them, talk about how you care about them, and tell the story about the time Jesus showed that he cared for his friends by washing their feet. This lays a foundation for caring.

With older children, you might use the story from chapter 13 of John, and then role-play by washing each other's feet. Most children will respond better if you use a lotion and massage the feet instead of washing them in water. Emphasize caring and set a serious tone.

Handicapping Conditions

To experience blindness, blindfold children or ask them to close their eyes, and then use a cane or yardstick to find a chair and sit down. Younger children may feel less threatened if they simply close their eyes. The children may also work with putting on or taking off a piece of clothing while blindfolded.

Older children can participate in a trust walk. Using partners, blindfold one child and have the partner lead the child on a walk through the building or onto the grounds. Partners then exchange roles.

For additional understanding opportunities, see "Experiencing Handicaps" in chapter 3.

Always follow up such experiences with a debriefing, asking those participating, as well as those observing and helping, how they felt during and after the experience.

News Alive!

Divide into groups. Each group looks through a newspaper and selects an article that tells of someone caring for others, then pantomimes the story or creates a human sculpture that depicts the news story. Then someone in the group tells briefly what is in the article. To do this in a shorter time, you could select several articles ahead of time and distribute them.

Open-ended Story

Give out slips of paper, each with a positive or negative answer response, such as:

- Ask for forgiveness.
- Ignore that person.

- Tell everyone else what happened.
- Tell a lie about what happened.
- Repay with a mean action.
- Offer forgiveness.

Tell a story of someone doing an unkind action to another person. Then stop the story and ask students to finish the story by following the instructions on their paper. Discuss what might happen if they actually did that. Discuss the best response and any additional good responses they might make.

Pantomime

Children take turns pantomiming some ways they can help others, and class members guess the act from their actions. Ahead of time, select common symbolic motions to indicate whether the act might be "at home," "at school," or "at church."

Puppets

Since our goal for using drama in Christian education is the experience of the participants, we need not have elaborate puppets such as those on TV or those sold in toy stores. Children enjoy puppets that are easily made, using a sock, a fabric cut with a simple head, arms, and body, or a paper bag. Try a new experience by bringing a sewing machine into the classroom to put together fabric puppets, after the children have drawn the faces and clothing with colored markers.

A simple face puppet, glued or stapled to the end of a craft stick or a strip of heavy cardboard, is appropriate for stories that express feelings. You might make one with a smiling face and one with a sad face, and the children can exchange the puppets, depending upon the feelings the story or discussion expresses.

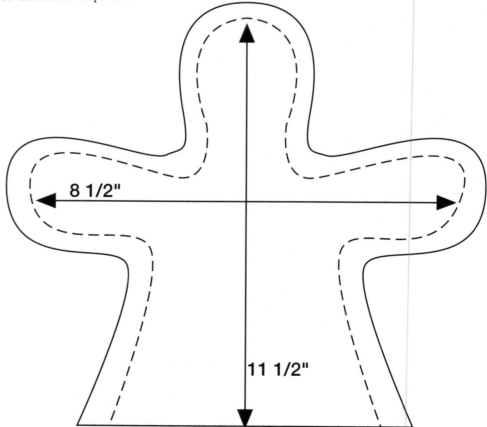

8 1/2"

11 1/2"

You also could make a hand puppet from a stuffed toy by opening a seam and removing the stuffing from the body, and a little from the head and arms (or front legs), to allow fingers to be used.

You need not have a puppet for every character in a story. In fact, you may prefer to simply use one puppet to tell the story. Many children will make up stories or express feelings about a situation when they can speak through the puppet, instead of saying it directly themselves. Give the child a puppet and ask him or her to have the puppet tell how it might have felt to be ignored in a group, or to be hungry or hurt. Or the child may pretend that the puppet "whispers" the information into the ear of the child, and the child speaks for the puppet.

If you plan to "act out" a story with puppets, turn a table on its side to become the stage. The children who work with the puppets sit on the floor behind the table and hold the puppets above the edge of the table. Or you might tie a rope across part of the room and drape a blanket over the rope, hiding the children as they manipulate the puppets above the blanket. Be certain that there is plenty of room behind the stage area for children to move about. Some of the purchased puppet stages can cause crowding if more than one or two children work behind them.

Role-playing

Through role-play, we step into the shoes (or role) of other people in a given situation. Older children particularly enjoy role-playing. Young children use a modified role-play during their own play, such as in homemaking and dress-up. This usually is done without even labeling it as role-play.

In the role-play, we either use a story to a certain point, and then ask the children to finish the story as they think the character(s) might have done it, or we give a specific situation or dilemma, and ask them to act out the way they would handle that situation.

Example 1: Jane has just moved to a big city from a very small town, where she knew everyone. Her school has more students than the total population of her previous town. At lunch, some students make fun of Jane's accent. Martha walks up to Jane and speaks. (Two people role-play a conversation between Jane and Martha.)

Example 2: Your Sunday school class decided to help a poor family have a nice Christmas. You promised to buy a gift for one of the children. As you and a friend are shopping, you see a special record you've been trying to find. Your friend tells you to buy the record, because you may not find it again. You have only enough money to buy either the gift or the record. (Act out what you would tell your friend and what you would do.)

Signing

Simple signing may be learned by all children. With preschool children, use only an occasional word. In fact, such words as *love, friend,* or *peace* might become methods of greeting your children. Older children can learn a complete song or reading. You might ask someone with signing experience to translate a song that you sing frequently. Then you could learn the signing, or arrange for the signer to teach the children. Or you could videotape the signer and use the tape to teach the children.

Signing has specific movements for specific words. Because it is the language for the hearing impaired, it should be learned correctly. Help the children distinguish between signing and creative movement. Your children will enjoy both experiences.

Stop-action Drama

A stop-action drama can be used with most stories. In this activity, students decide on ways to show a part of the story in still-life scenes that stop the action. As an example, the story of the good Samaritan can be stopped when the robbers beat up the traveler; when the church officials pass by; when the Samaritan is treating the traveler; and at the inn. Allow the children to decide how they might stage a still-life scene for each situation. After planning the scenes, go through the story a time or two, moving into the scenes automatically when you come to the stop in the story.

Afterward, ask participants to show how they felt during their still-life scenes.

Teaching Through Storytelling

Since the beginning of time, storytelling has held peoples and meanings together. Storytelling helps us live through other people's situations and develop understanding through their experiences.

Books

As you read children's books, be alert for ways they can be used to help children learn to care for God's people. The book need not necessarily be a religious book. Consider *Benjamin Brody's Backyard Bag* by Phyllis Vos Wezeman. The boy in the story has a special bag and learns how homeless people use bags. Help children realize that there are many reasons for homelessness. It might be due to fire or illness, mental retardation with no one who cares, divorce or abuse, unemployment, lack of housing, or rent increase.

Older elementary children will enjoy Dr. Seuss's *The Butter Battle Book*. After reading it, discuss such questions as:

- What caused the conflict?
- How did it become worse?
- Where did the cooperation between people begin to break down?
- How did it turn out?
- How could the results have come about in a better way?

Make Up Stories

Collect pictures from magazines that show persons in conflict and others that show persons caring for one another. Encourage children to make up stories about what might be going on in the picture and how the people might feel. Consider audiotaping the stories as the children tell them and sharing the taped stories with other classes.

Oral Histories/Stories

Locate people who have lived in other countries and audiotape stories they can share. Include stories about customs, as well as traditional stories from those countries.

Shared Storytelling

For children who can read, mix up parts of a story about stewardship, then have each child read the section he or she has found.
- Write sections of a story on strips of paper and insert each strip into a balloon. Standing in a circle, toss the balloons back and forth. At a signal, each person takes a balloon and

pops it. Then the children read their section of the story to themselves and find where they fit into the story according to the other children's strips of paper. When all have found their places, read the story aloud in sections.

- Write sections of a story on strips of paper, number them, then mix them up and pass them out. Children then arrange themselves in the order of the story.
- Write sections of a story on strips of paper for a treasure hunt. On the back of each strip, write a clue to where the next section of the story may be found.

Storytellers

Many communities have a Storyteller's Guild. Check your local library for information. Where possible, locate people with cultural traditions other than those of your children.

Arrange for a storytelling workshop and develop a storytelling group within your own church.

Becoming a Storyteller

Jesus based many of his teachings on stories, and he must have been good at it, because people spent hours listening to him. Anyone can tell a story, but storytelling is an art that most of us must develop. The way we tell a story makes a difference in the way it is received.

Turn to Luke 12:13-21 and read the story of the "rich fool" twice. The first time, read verse 20 as if God were passing judgment. The second time, read it with compassion. As you will see, without the tone of the storyteller's voice, we do not comprehend the full meaning of the story.

All stories contain plot, place, and persons. Like the legs of a milking stool, we need all three to make the story complete. We often think of the plot as the most important, but sometimes the plot is developed only to tell about the person or the place. Without the descriptive words, a story falls flat.

The following suggestions will help you learn a story:

1. Identify the four parts of the story (introduction, plot, climax, ending).
2. Get to know the characters, the customs of the time and area, and the location of the story.
3. Think about how the listener will relate to the characters and situations in the story.
4. Divide the story into blocks. Concentrate on each block, and look at the connecting words between the blocks. Concentrate on the beginning and end of each block, then on the whole story.
5. Repeat the story several times, "thinking" it as you speak. You will want to internalize the story—help it "leave" the page and become a part of you. Some people find it helpful to use a tape recorder as they practice. A storytelling partner will also help. Consider these suggestions as you tell the story:
   a. A well-told story is better than a well-read story, but a well-read story is far better than a poorly told story. The key lies in knowing the story so well that it becomes a part of you, whether you tell it or read it. If you use the book only in order to follow the sequence, then write the sequence on a large sheet of paper and post it high on the wall above the listeners' heads. You will remember the sequence more easily if you practice it in blocks.
   b. Consider any props and gestures you plan to use. These enhance the story. But any story should always be told as if the listeners could not see the props and gestures. Use only appropriate gestures. In the story of Jesus healing the paralytic, Jesus asked the scribes, "Why do you raise such questions in your hearts?" If an accusing, pointing gesture is used, one message will be conveyed. But if a gesture of opening

the hands in puzzlement is used, then we see Jesus' question in another light, as concern over the scribes' attitude (Mark 2:1-12). Which attitude stands more in keeping with Jesus' life and teachings?

    c. Think about your tone of voice, facial expressions, and body posture. Happiness comes about through the tone as well as the words.

    d. Don't avoid pauses. Pauses give us time to think. They allow space in our thoughts for setting the stage.

  6. Relax and enjoy the story. You will find that storytelling can bring you as much joy as it brings the listeners.

(These suggestions adapted from Delia Halverson, *How to Train Volunteer Teachers* [Nashville: Abingdon Press, 1991], Handout 12.)

Storytelling may be biblical, historical, or modern day. To help children learn to care for God's people, use stories from other cultures or stories that exemplify our calling to act as God's stewards. Include historical and contemporary stories about persons in mission, both employed and volunteer. Older children will enjoy stories of heroes from other countries. Two stories are included in this chapter, but you can find a wealth of stories in other resources.

The Jug of Water

A Nigerian tribal chief sent out his messengers to invite all the men of the tribe to a great feast. "All the food will be provided," they announced, "but each man must bring one jug of palm wine."

Ezra wanted to attend the great festival very much, but he had no wine. He paced the floor, trying to think of a solution for his dilemma. Finally his wife suggested, "You could buy a jug of wine. It is not too expensive for such a great occasion."

"How foolish," Ezra cried, "to spend money when there is a way to go free." Once again he paced until he came upon a plan. "Rather than wine, I will carry water in my jug. Several hundred men will attend the festival. What will it hurt to add one jug of water to the great pot of wine?"

On the day of the feast, the tribal drums began to beat early in the morning, reminding the people of the great festival. All the men came dressed in their finest clothes, and gathered by midmorning at the home of the chief. As each man entered the tribal grounds, he poured his jug of wine into a large earthen pot. Ezra carefully poured the contents of his container into the pot, greeted the chief, and joined the dancers.

When all the guests arrived, the chief commanded the music to cease and ordered the servants to fill everyone's glass with wine. As the chief spoke the opening words of the festival, all the guests raised their glasses and drank. Suddenly a cry of disbelief arose from the crowd, and they quickly drank again. What they tasted was not wine, but water. Each guest had decided that his one jug of water could not spoil the great pot of palm wine.

(William R. White, *Stories for Telling* [Minneapolis: Augsburg Press, 1986], p. 66. This story was adapted from an African folktale.)

It's Not My Job!

Our story opens on the road from a neighborhood elementary school to a nearby football field. Bubba, a typical fun-loving student, has gone for a walk. As he walks along, he can be heard whistling a happy tune. Then he begins to skip and jump. "What a great day!" he exclaims.

Just then three robbers, looking incredibly mean, jump out from behind a tree. "Oh no!" shouts Bubba. "I saw you last week in the principal's office."

"That's right!" the robbers exclaim in unison. "We're the Bully family—Bully #1, #2, and #3!" With that, they begin to beat up poor Bubba. Bully #1 kicks him. Bully #2 hits him. Bully #3 taunts him, "Nah-nah-nah-nah-nah, nah!" They take his lunchbox and go, leaving Bubba half-dead in the gutter.

A few minutes later, a local religious leader, Charlie Churchperson, happens down that same road. He sees Bubba lying in the gutter and says, "Oh dear. There's someone who needs help." He walks a little closer and sees that Bubba is in bad shape. "I can't help him," he says. "I might get my hands dirty." So Charlie Churchperson moves to the other side of the road and says, "It's not my job!" (The audience boos!)

A few moments later, along comes another leader, Terry the Teacher. She sees Bubba and thinks, "Boy, he's in bad shape." She pauses for a few seconds, and then crosses to the other side of the road, saying, "It's not my job!" (The audience boos!)

The next person to come along is a student from a rival elementary school, heading for home with her dog—a huge Saint Bernard. This student's name is G. Samaritan, and her dog's name, curiously enough, is Dog. Soon, G. Samaritan sees Bubba by the road and realizes right away Bubba needs help. Now, students from these two schools don't like one another at all. But that doesn't matter to G. Samaritan. "This guy needs help," she says. "It's my job to take care of him!" (The audience cheers!)

She puts her coat over Bubba and puts him on her dog, Dog. They carry Bubba to the nearest Holiday Inn, and G. pays them to take care of Bubba and call his parents.

The Bully family is caught eating Bubba's lunch and is sent to the principal's office once again. Bubba survives and loves to tell people how he was rescued by G. Samaritan. "I know that G. stands for Good," says Bubba. G. Samaritan has shown what being a good neighbor is all about!

(*Upper-Elementary Meetings* [Loveland, Col.: Group Publishing, Copyright © 1989 by Thom Schultz Publications, Inc.], p. 104.)

Teaching Through Reflection

In our world of music, television, and action-packed schedules, we seldom take time to simply sit back and reflect. We condition our children to think that every void must be filled from without. They have little opportunity to fill their voids by listening to God's voice within themselves.

The following experiences will help children reflect. Do not be afraid to allow silent times for reflection. God cannot talk to us when our minds try to fill up every void moment.

Borrowed Items

Reflect on and/or discuss the situations below:

- How would you feel if your little sister drew on your mother's library book, and your mother made you buy a new one?
- How would you feel if you marked on your own library book, and you asked your mother to pay for a new one?
- How would you feel if your friend borrowed your roller blades and left them outside, and the friend's dog chewed them up?
- How would you feel if you left your own roller blades outside and your dog chewed them up?

How should we treat borrowed things? Read Psalm 24:1. What does it say about the ownership of the world?

Create Order Out of Chaos

This is appropriate for older children. Before class time, create chaos in the classroom by upsetting the chairs and tables, moving things out of place, throwing "clean" trash on the floor, and so on. Leave an area open near the door so that all of you can sit together on the floor. Close the blinds or cover the windows, and turn off the light. Meet your students outside the classroom and read (or have a student read) the first chapter of Genesis. Then take the children into the classroom and sit together on the floor in the dark.

Recall that before creation, the world was without light, was void of life, and without form. Then ask the students if they remember what God did the first day of creation. When someone responds, "Light," flood the room with lights. Ask the students how the room is different. Talk about the definition of *chaos* in comparison to *order*. As the class goes about setting order to the room, talk about the order that God has established in the universe, that one thing depends on another, and some things are becoming extinct or damaged because of the upset of balance. Discuss our stewardship responsibility to maintain the balance God created.

Creating Something Special

Guide children's thoughts by asking them to close their eyes and think as you read the following:

Imagine that you have a special mission. You are about to create the most beautiful thing in the world. Think what that special thing might be. (Pause) All right, now keep that in your mind and imagine that you are creating it. (Pause) Imagine the care that you take as you make it. (Pause)

Now, it's all made. Imagine that you place it on a shelf in front of you and look at it. Isn't it wonderful? (Pause) Suddenly you think that something might happen to it. What do you suppose might happen to it? (Pause)

You really don't want anything to happen to it, so who might you get to take care of it? (Pause) Think about the person you would ask to care for it. That person would be your steward. Do you think he or she would understand how important this creation is to you? (Pause)

God made something special when God made the world. Here is what the psalmist said about how God found someone to take care of this special creation:

> *You have given them dominion over the works of your hands;*
> *you have put all things under their feet.* (Psalm 8:6)

Tell the children to open their eyes and talk about how they felt about their great creations, and their fear of having them destroyed. Remind them that we are stewards of God's earth.

The Whole Elephant

Draw an elephant on a poster board, or mount a picture of an elephant on a large piece of heavy-weight paper. Cut the elephant apart into legs, tusks, a trunk, a tail, a stomach, ears, and so on, and give a piece to each student.

Ask the students to imagine that they have never seen an elephant and that they are blind. Ask them to describe what they would think about the elephant if they could only feel the part of the elephant on their picture.

After your discussion, read the following poem to the children. Then talk about the importance of knowing everything possible about people before we judge them.

The Blind Men and the Elephant

It was six men of Indostan
   To learning much inclined,
Who went to see the Elephant
   (Though all of them were blind),
That each by observation
   Might satisfy his mind.

The *First* approached the Elephant,
   And happening to fall
Against his broad and sturdy side,
   At once began to bawl:
"God bless me! But the Elephant
   Is very like a wall!"

The *Second*, feeling of the tusk,
   Cried, "Ho! what have we here
So very round and smooth and sharp?
   To me 'tis mighty clear
This wonder of an Elephant
   Is very like a spear!"

The *Third* approached the animal,
   And, happening to take
The squirming trunk within his hands,
   Thus boldly up and spake:
"I see," quoth he, "the Elephant
   Is very like a snake!"

The *Fourth* reached out an eager hand,
   And felt about the knee.
"What most this wondrous beast is like
   Is mighty plain," quoth he;
" 'Tis clear enough the Elephant
   Is very like a tree!"

The *Fifth*, who chanced to touch the ear,
   Said: "E'en the blindest man
Can tell what this resembles most;
   Deny the fact who can,
This marvel of an Elephant
   Is very like a fan!"

The *Sixth* no sooner had begun
   About the beast to grope,
Than, seizing on the swinging tail
   That fell within his scope,
"I see," quoth he, "the Elephant
   Is very like a rope!"

And so these men of Indostan
   Disputed loud and long,
Each in his own opinion
   Exceeding stiff and strong,
Though each was partly in the right,
   And all were in the wrong!

So oft in theologic wars,
   The disputants, I ween,
Rail on in utter ignorance
   Of what each other mean,
And prate about an Elephant
   Not one of them has seen!

John Godfrey Saxe

Fable of Sticks

Collect small sticks, all about the same size and small enough for a child to break. You could use craft sticks for this. You will need two sticks per child.

Give each child two sticks, and ask them to break one stick.

Say, "I wonder what will happen if we combine our sticks." Collect the second stick from each child and make a bundle, binding them with a string or rubber band. Pass the bundle around the class, challenging the children to try to break the sticks now. Then read the following old fable.

Seven Sticks

There was once a man who had seven sons. But the seven began to quarrel among themselves. The father wondered if there would ever be peace in his household.

One day the old man called his seven sons together. To each, he gave a single stick, saying, "Break it." Each son took the stick he was offered and broke it quickly.

Then the father took seven more sticks. These he bound tightly together with cord to form a neat, tight bundle. Now, in turn, he handed the bundle to each son with the command, "Break it!"

Each son took the bundle of seven sticks eagerly, intent upon this new show of strength. But though they strained greatly, there was not one who could break the bundle when all were bound together.

So it was that the seven sons learned to live in peace.

(*Middle Elementary Student*, Summer 1981 [Nashville: Graded Press], p. 24.)

Footsteps of Another

Ask the children to reflect on what it might feel like to be:

- the oldest child in a family
- the middle child in a family
- the youngest child in a family
- the only child in a family
- the oldest adult in the church family
- someone who doesn't know anyone else in church
- someone who has no living relatives at all
- someone whose relatives all live far away at Thanksgiving, Christmas, other holidays
- someone whose house and everything in it has just burned
- someone who has never learned to read even the simplest street sign

Hunger Deaths

Cut out three sets of 28 "people" (84 in all). Cut each set of 28 from a different color of construction paper.

Sit in a circle and hand out the "people" around the class until they are all distributed. Explain that these paper "people" represent the number of persons who die every three minutes due to hunger-related causes. Tell the children that you will use a timer (or large clock with a minute hand), and during the first minute on the timer, all paper "people" of the first color (state color) will be thrown into the middle of the circle, representing the number who died that minute. The next color will be thrown the second minute, and the third color the third minute. Have complete quiet during this time. The ticking of a timer makes it more dramatic.

After the experience, talk about how the children felt as they thought of each person dying of hunger. Was it difficult to throw their "person" into the center?

Methuselah, the Tree

Reproduce the page showing the cross section of a tree. Give each child a copy and a pencil, and ask them to think about your words as you tell them about the tree, Methuselah, and to follow your instructions. Read the following, pausing for them to write their thoughts on the tree rings. After you finish, their papers may be used as their dedication to act as stewards and care for God's people.

My name is Methuselah. I am a bristlecone pine more than 4,600 years old, one of the world's oldest known living things. I grow in the Inyo National Forest in the White Mountains of California. I'm bent by the winds that have blown all these years, telling me of the many changes in our world.

You may think I'm old, but many, many years ago, even before I sprouted from a seed, God set this earth into systems so that all the world works together. Sometimes you humans call the systems that God set up *ecosystems*. Look at your picture of my rings, and in the ring closest to the center, write the sentence, "Ecosystems created by God." That's spelled e-c-o-s-y-s-t-e-m-s. This happened before I sprouted from a seed. **(Pause)**

You see, a part of the ecosystem includes the way you humans must have oxygen to breathe, and we trees must produce oxygen as we grow. We are all in this together, making the world function in the way God planned.

As I grow, each year I put on a new ring. Look for the wide ring closest to the center ring. That represents the ring that grew when I was well over a thousand years old. That is when someone wrote the book in the Bible called Genesis. The writer wrote that God created human beings in God's own image. God gave to the Hebrews, and to all people who come after them, dominion over the earth. Dominion over something does not mean that you can use it any way you want, but it means that you must be responsible for it. That makes you stewards of the earth and all that is in it. Write in that ring, "Writer of Genesis tells us that people are stewards for God." **(Pause)**

People did not always care for the earth. The next ring represents the time Moses taught the people to care for God's earth by letting the land rest one year in seven. Write in that ring, "Moses tells us to give the land rest one year in seven." **(Pause)**

The next large ring represents the years that King David lived. He wrote many psalms about the earth. One of them says, "The earth is the Lord's and all that is in it, the world, and those who live in it" (Psalm 24:1). In that ring, write, "David tells us the earth belongs to the Lord." **(Pause)**

You will find one more large ring in your picture. That ring represents the years that Jesus lived on earth and taught care for the earth and the people. Write in that ring, "Jesus taught to care for God's people." **(Pause)** In order to care for God's people, you must care for the earth, so that God's people have a good place to live.

You will see many tiny rings between the ring for Jesus' life and the outside of my trunk. In those years, some folks have cared for the earth and God's people, and some folks haven't. The space closest to the bark on my trunk represents this year. If you want to be a steward for God and care for God's people, write in that ring, "I will be a steward and care for God's people." **(Pause)**

(Adapted from Delia Halverson, "Methuselah," *New Call to Mission—Planting Trees to Reclaim God's Earth* [Nashville: Graded Press].)

Methuselah, the Tree

Native Americans

After a study of Native American people, such as *Crickets and Corn* by Peg Back, use the following with older elementary children, reflecting on the common beliefs, rather than differences. Talk about how Jesus did not insist that people of other cultures practice his cultural traditions in order to accept God. He simply told them of God's love. (See "Foreign" Image in chapter 2). *Brother Eagle, Sister Sky*, by Susan Jeffers, lifts up our common theology of stewardship.

> Long before my people journeyed to this land your people were here,
> and you received from your elders an understanding of creation,
> and of the Mystery that surrounds us all,
> that was deep, and rich and to be treasured.
> We did not hear you when you shared your vision.
> In our zeal to tell you of the good news of Jesus Christ,
> we were closed to the value of your spirituality.
> We confused western ways and culture with the depth and breadth
> and the length and height of the gospel of Christ.
> We imposed our civilization as a condition of accepting the gospel.
> We tried to make you be like us, and in so doing
> we helped to destroy the vision that made you what you were.
> As a result you, and we, are poorer,
> and the image of the Creator in us is twisted, blurred,
> and we are not what we are meant by God to be.
> We ask you to forgive us, and we ask you to walk with us in the Spirit of Christ,
> so that our peoples may be blessed and God's creation healed.

(Apology to Native Congregations, given by United Church of Canada General Council to Native Elders. From "Gathering into the Sacred Circle," *The Whole People of God, Unit 1* [Inver Grove Hgts., Minn.: Logos Productions, Inc., 1986], pp. 1-8.)

Pro- or Anti-earth

Ask the class:

- How many of you are pro-earth?
- How many of you are anti-earth?

Brainstorm where and how people might picket if they are anti-earth. Examples might be slogans such as "Stop this senseless recycling!" or "Waste more!" or "Cut all trees! Destroy oxygen!"

Scripture Doodles

Give each child crayons and paper. Ask them to "doodle" their thoughts during the reading of a section of scripture, and then share their doodle thoughts with the whole group.

Use such scriptures as Matthew 25:34-40; Genesis 1:1-27; Mark 12:29-31; John 15:12-17; I Corinthians 13; or Romans 12:1-8. If you use a shorter passage, you may want to repeat it in order to give ample time for reflection.

Talents

Ahead of time, ask a student to prepare to read I Corinthians 12:12-27 to the group.

For this meditation, ask the students to get into a comfortable position and close their eyes as you help them think about their own special talent. Use the following words:

Imagine that you are in a special place where you like to go alone. It may be in your home, or it may be outside. Think about what your place looks like. What makes it so special? **(Pause)**

Now think about yourself. Where is the really-really *me* part of yourself? Is the really-really you your arm? Is it your foot? Is it your head? What part of you laughs and cries? What part of you loves, and what part feels great when you do something for someone else? That part is the really-really you. **(Pause)**

Now, take the really-really you part of you deep inside yourself. Take it into your heart. **(Pause)** Invite God to come into your heart. Invite God to come into your heart with the really-really you. **(Pause)** Show God some special thing about yourself. It may be something special that you can do or make, or something you are especially good at in school, or it may be some special way you treat others. **(Pause)**

Remember that God made you special. God made you with that special talent. God planned for you to be special in that way. **(Pause)** Thank God for giving you that special talent. **(Pause)**

Ask God to help you find ways to use your special talent. It may be at home, at school, at church, or in the community. It may be with your family, with your friends, or with someone you don't know. **(Pause)**

If you don't know right now just when or how you will use your talent, know that God will show you just how when the time comes. You'll know inside yourself. **(Pause)** When you are ready, you may open your eyes.

Tell the young people that Paul wrote about the special talents that each of us has, and that all of those talents are important to the whole body of Christ, just as each part of the body is important to a person. Ask the student who prepared earlier to read I Corinthians 12:12-27.

(Adapted from Delia Halverson, *Teaching Prayer in the Classroom* [Nashville: Abingdon Press, 1989], pp. 39-40).

Talents and Popcorn

First read Matthew 25:35-40. Then give everyone a hard kernel of popcorn. Talk about how small and hard it is and that it doesn't appear to be good to eat. Pop the corn together. Then ask the students to reflect on the ways popcorn is like their talents.

Example: When exposed to heat it explodes and becomes a soft, velvety treat, smooth to the tongue and pleasant to eat. When we allow God to heat us in service, our small, seemingly insignificant talents expand and explode for others.

(Note: It is fun to spread a clean sheet on the floor and place an open corn popper in the center, allowing the corn to pop high and onto the sheet.)

Treasured Possessions

Ask students to list five of their most treasured possessions. Then ask these questions:

- What might you have done with the money you spent on some of your possessions, if you had not bought them?
- What would you do with the time you spend with those possessions, if you did not have them?
- Go back and think about each possession individually, as I ask a question.
- Think of the first possession on your list. Does this cause you *not* to follow Christ to your best ability? **(Pause)**

- Think of the second (third, fourth, fifth) on your list. Does this cause you *not* to follow Christ to your best ability? **(Pause)**

You might follow these questions by asking each child to make a written commitment to use one possession differently in the future.

Example: Some may spend all their money on cassette tapes or special clothes, and give none to special projects for the church. Or they may spend all their time looking at videos, and have no time to help someone who needs them.

TV Commercials

Children think literally, and they tend to believe everything the "authorities" tell them. Consequently, they look at TV commercials as an authority.

Videotape several commercials to show the class. After each commercial, ask such questions as:

- Do you think those shoes made the person run fast, or did he/she practice running?
- When they show a person very happy while driving a car, does it mean that you will always be happy when you get in the car and drive?
- When the person uses that particular fragrance and all the women (or men) turn and follow, does that mean that all you need to do is buy that fragrance, and everyone will like you?

Talk about why companies make commercials and air them on TV. (Basically, to convince you that you cannot live without their product and must purchase it.) Talk about the difference between needs and wants. (See "Distinguish Between Needs and Wants" in chapter 3.)

Develop a checklist of questions to ask yourself while watching TV. The list might include:

- ✓ What is the commercial really telling me?
- ✓ If I had this, what difference would it make in my life?
- ✓ Is this something I need, or something I want?
- ✓ How long will this (or the pleasure from it) last?
- ✓ What will I need to give up in order to purchase this?
- ✓ What else could I purchase for myself with the same amount of money?
- ✓ What could I do for others with the same amount of money?
- ✓ What would God like me to do about purchasing this?

TV and Movie Violence and Consequences

Many of today's movies and TV shows actually block our consciousness of caring acts by not showing the consequences of violence.

I first recognized this several years ago when I saw *Raiders of the Lost Ark*, which included a comical vehicle chase through the streets of Spain. The people along the sidewalk, even those on ladders, working on the side of a building, were knocked aside by the rushing cars. It was a hilarious chase, and the person with me, who had seen the movie before, wanted to see it again because of his interest in those carrying out the stunt roles.

As the audience moved on down the road and across a mountain, along with the chase on the screen, my mind remained back in the town, with the people who had fallen from the ladders. We never knew what consequences the chase caused the bystanders. We were left with no concern in our hearts for those knocked out of the roadway, bounced off the fenders, falling from ladders. How can we expect children who watch such acts to develop an understanding of the consequences of their actions and a sense of caring?

Older elementary children can spend some time reflecting on such actions. Videotape scenes from various TV shows that ignore the consequences to bystanders and show them to the students. Stop the tape after the action and reflect on what might have happened to the bystanders, and how they might feel. Talk about how the characters in the show might react in a caring way. This will raise the children's consciousness when viewing such scenes and help them to overcome the numbing effect that such shows have on our caring nature.

Your class may want to write a complaint to the TV producers and commercial sponsors, or to the stations carrying the programs. Point out that such a letter is not only a caring act, but also good stewardship of TV.

Teaching Through Writing and Research

6 I don't recall a single creative-writing assignment in any of my formal schooling. Consequently, it never occurred to me to write out my thoughts, and it was not until my children were half grown that I realized how writing could clear my thoughts. Once I put it on paper, then I begin to see just what I'm thinking.

I encourage you to help children with writing skills to record their thoughts. Younger children will need to voice their thoughts for adults to write, but even if they cannot read it, they thrill to see their thoughts in writing.

All children can deal with some sort of research projects. Preschoolers will need to work with research that does not require reading, or where reading can be done by adults, with the children deciding what will be included in the report.

As we work with children on writing or research assignments, we must recognize that we do not teach grammar and composition in Christian education. Our time is far too precious to spend it on such goals. The school system is responsible for that. We must work with the skills that children attain elsewhere. Instead, we use writing and research as a tool, to help children record good ideas and the way they think and feel inside.

Assure your children that they need to write only in a form that they can read themselves. If you later plan to print something for others to read, then you may help the child edit it for publication.

Writing assignments can be approached in various ways. Too often we make writing "copy" assignments, giving children certain verses on various themes to copy on paper. This does not create learning. Instead, it creates boredom. Writing assignments need to be creative. They must involve thought about the subject. The learning comes through the experience, and that experience is more pleasurable when done in cooperation with others. Therefore, unless it's a personal reflection experience, I work on writing assignments as a large group or in small groups. Working in groups also helps remove the competitive attitude. Children in your class will have a variety of reading and writing levels, and all of them will be more able to participate when they work in groups.

The experiences in this chapter deal primarily with elementary children because of their ability to read and write. However, preschoolers may participate in some of the research projects that do not require reading, or in which the reading can be done by adults, letting the children decide what to include in the "report."

Write Worship Expressions

Arrange with the pastor for your class to write some part of the liturgy for a Sunday worship. Consider one of these:

- a creed stating belief of equality of persons, or stewardship of time, talents, money, or our environment.
- an offertory prayer, thanking God for the gift of money, and dedicating our gifts back to God.
- a poem stressing how people depend upon nature and nature depends upon people.
- paraphrase (see chapter 8) a scripture on stewardship, or caring for others.

Poetry

Poetry sounds foreign to most of us, but actually, inside all of us, hide a poet's thoughts. Some styles of poetry appeal to some children, while others will grasp another style. Experiment with several styles at different times. You may discover that one style is more popular with your children than another. You will need to keep aware of new students coming into your class and offer them an opportunity to try different styles.

Never just tell children to "write a poem" about something. Give them direction for one style or another. Below are the three forms I most frequently use:

1. *Picture poems* use words or phrases to outline the shape of a symbol or object. The words may express feelings or thoughts about the subject.

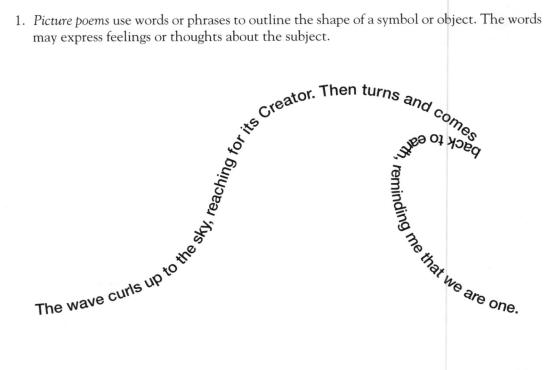

2. *Cinquain* (sin-cane) poetry is not as complicated as it sounds and gives structure to creative thinking. A thesaurus sometimes helps older children, but do not rely on it. The cinquain poem has five lines, using this formula:

Line 1: One-word title or subject.
Line 2: Two words that tell about the subject. These words may compose a phrase, or they may be separate words.
Line 3: Three verbs or action words (such as "ing" words), or a three-word phrase about the subject.
Line 4: Four words that tell of the writer's feelings about the subject.
Line 5: The subject word again, or another word that refers back to the title or subject. If the poem is a prayer, this word may be "Amen." *Example*:

Hunger

no   food

pain   dizziness   stumbling

I cannot even think.

Help!

3. *Free verse* takes various forms. It may include phrases, sentences, or a series of words. The lines may vary in length, and the words may or may not rhyme. Action words give excitement to the poem. *Examples:*

The earth is the Lord's
        the trees, the ocean, the shore.
The earth is the Lord's,
        laughing water, screaming wind, and more.
God gave me a charge
        to know, to care, to love.
As steward I work for all,
        on earth and also above.

I Have a Dream

I have a dream . . .
That the American government will be better
    and help the poor people
        and help the children be treated better
            and help people get nice homes like I have.
I have a dream . . .
    That all people will be equal
        and will not fight one another
            and that women get treated better in some places.
I have a dream . . .
    That all people remember Martin Luther King
        as a great man.

                    Amy Thandiwe Gobledale, 2nd Grade,
                    West Franklin, New Hampshire

(Excerpt from *Skipping Stones*, Vol. 4, p. 29)

Pen Pals

Personal or class pen pals may be set up. Contact your church mission organization for churches in other countries for your class to write to. Your class may want to exchange items that are typical of each country.

For individual pen pals, write to *Skipping Stones* (A Multicultural Children's Quarterly), P.O. Box 3939, Eugene OR 97403; tel. 503-342-4956. (Unless you are a subscriber or of low-income, there is a $5.00 charge for listing on the Pen Pal Page, but paying a fee carries a commitment to follow up.)

Scale of Giving

Draw a big scale on a large piece of paper. Give children small papers cut in the shape of weights. On each paper "weight," they write reasons for giving. Then as a group, discuss the different reasons and tape them on the plus or minus side of the scale, depending upon whether you decide it is a Christian's attitude for giving. Some of the reasons may be:

- Give to church because parents tell you to.
- Give to a friend because he/she will give to you.
- Give because you desire to help others.
- Give to someone because you know it will make that person happy.
- Give to a TV ministry because the evangelist cries, and his voice "moves you" and you are sorry for him.
- Give because someone has told you that you will go to hell if you don't give.
- Give so that God will love you.
- Give because you love God.
- Give because you feel privileged to give as a Christian.
- Give because you recognize that all that you have is actually God's.

Finish your discussion by reading Matthew 6:1-4.

Research Favorite Possessions

Prepare papers for each child in the following manner:

Beginning at the bottom of the page, turn up two inches of paper four times, leaving a three-inch area at the top. In that area, write "My Favorite Possessions," and draw a line along the top fold.

Unfold one section and draw a line along the top of that fold. Write in that area, "Favorite Possession #1."

Unfold the next section and draw a line along top of fold. Write in that area, "Favorite Possession #2."

Unfold next section and draw a line along top of fold. Write in that area, "Favorite Possession #3."

Unfold last section and draw a line along fold line. Write in that area, "Favorite Possession #4."

Refold bottom fold (covering up possession #4), and write on reverse side of page that is folded over, "How I would feel if I could not have possession #4."

Refold next fold (covering up possession #3), and write on reverse side of page that is folded over, "How I would feel if I could not have possession #3."

Refold next fold (covering up possession #2), and write on reverse side of page that is folded over, "How I would feel if I could not have possession #2."

Refold last fold (covering up possession #1), and write on reverse side of page that is folded over, "How I would feel if I could not have possession #1."

Open all the sheets flat and give a sheet to each child. Ask the children to think about all the things they own personally, and then ask that they decide on their four favorite possessions. They then write these in the four sections indicated. When all have finished, ask them to turn up the first fold, covering up possession #4. Ask them to think about losing that possession, and then answer the question on the folded paper. Continue with all four possessions.

Ask the children to turn their folded paper over and answer these questions on the back:

- What makes it possible for me to have these possessions? (parents, gifts from others, my job, and so on)
- Why are my parents (or why am I) able to work to have money to buy these possessions? (God gave us ability/brains/talents/opportunities.)
- How can I be a good steward of these possessions?

Talk together about their answers.

Research Litter

Give each child a plastic bag and a plastic glove. Take everyone out on the lawn (or other designated area) and fill the bags with trash or litter of any kind. Tell the children to be careful when picking up sharp objects.

After five or ten minutes, bring everyone together (inside or out) and separate the litter into two piles: "natural" litter (dead leaves, branches, and such) and "people" litter (plastic cups, drink cans, paper, and such). Ask the children to study what they have gathered. Use the following questions for discussion:

- Which pile is larger?
- Does any of the litter harm our environment in any way? How?
- Does the litter cause sight pollution (unsightly things we see)?
- If any of the litter harms our environment, how can we reduce the harm it does?
- If it takes 1,000 gallons of water to produce aluminum for one can, how much water did you save by recycling the cans you found?

Write for Action

Write to businesses, objecting to their advertising or products. United Methodists in Boston convinced the Converse Shoe Company that "Run 'N Gun" was the wrong name for a sneaker. Although the name comes from a basketball term, with today's use of firearms by children, the company was convinced to change the sneaker name to "Run 'N Slam." Although this protest was spearheaded by adults, much of advertising now aims its efforts toward children, recognizing that parents buy what the children want. Therefore, they now listen to the voices of children even more than in the past.

Children can research fast-food restaurants in your community to see which are using recyclable products. They may write to those that do not, telling them they will ask their parents to use another restaurant unless they switch their practice.

Another research may be done by asking each child to collect the packaging on everything coming into the house from the store for a week. Measure and weigh the amount of packaging, then write to the companies concerned, telling them of your findings and urging them to reduce their packaging.

Write to government or church officials, with supportive suggestions and informed criticism about their actions toward others. When writing, be brief, courteous, and specific about your information or complaint. The letter should be personal and be neatly handwritten or typed. Using form letters is usually a waste of time.

Address Senators:	The Honorable_____
	U.S. Senate
	Washington DC 20510
Address Representatives:	The Honorable_____
	U.S. House of Representatives
	Washington DC 20515

Inheritance

This research can be carried out by children who have a basic working knowledge of math. Use the following situation problem to talk about how we use our money as God's stewards:

There was a father who had two children. He said, "I want to give you an inheritance. I can give it to you in either of two ways, and you must choose which way you want to receive it.
1. I will give you a million dollars right now, for you to do with as you please.
2. I will give you one cent today, and double it every month for three years.
*   Which do you choose?"*

Have the children decide immediately which they would choose. Then have them work the problem and see if they still feel right about their choice.
(Note: In solving this problem, we can forget that the recipient in the second case receives double each month, but still has what was given in the previous months. The second choice receives the most money: $20.48 the first year; $83,886.08 the second year; and $343,597,3873.70 the third year.)

As you debrief, talk about making good use of all that God has given us by planning carefully. Use these passages, along with a discussion on the way we use our money: Matthew 6:24; Luke 12:31-34; and I John 3:17. Help the children realize that we do not want to make money in order to possess it, but rather to be able to use it in caring for God's people.

Research Newspapers

Search through newspapers for stories of people who have acted in caring ways for others. Create a caring bulletin board with these stories. You might title the bulletin board "God's People Care." Place the bulletin board where it can be seen by the whole church family.

OR

Select newspaper stories that (1) promote good feelings (peace) among people and (2) promote bad feelings (animosity) between persons. Discuss why more bad news than good news is reported, and how we can help to change this. Use Isaiah 2:4 and Matthew 5:9 in the discussion.

Research Careers

Older children are not yet ready to make career choices, but it is not too early to plant seeds of ways that careers reflect our dedication to caring for God's people.

First, spend some time simply listing careers in which persons care for God's people, and careers that can be harmful to God's people.

Then decide which careers you may want to feature in a booklet with information about various careers that help God's people. Assign different groups of children to research these careers, using books from the library or interviewing persons in those careers. Your local library will have a variety of books on different careers. Don't forget such careers as nurses, teachers, physical therapists, child care helpers, and so on.

You might specifically locate *The Complete Guide to Environmental Careers*, published by Environmental Careers Organization, 286 Congress St., Dept. GM, Boston MA 02210, tel. 617-426-4375. Many people do not realize that *Peterson's Guide to Four Year Colleges* includes 40 different academic majors that involve the environment. For mission career information, contact your denominational headquarters or Church World Service, P.O. Box 968, Elkhart IN 46515.

Clues to Kindness

Reproduce copies of the magnifying glass outline below. Send copies of these home with the children. As the children act out a kindness to others, they fill in the clue and ask the person to whom the kindness was acted to sign the magnifying glass. Preschool children can participate in this with the help of parents.

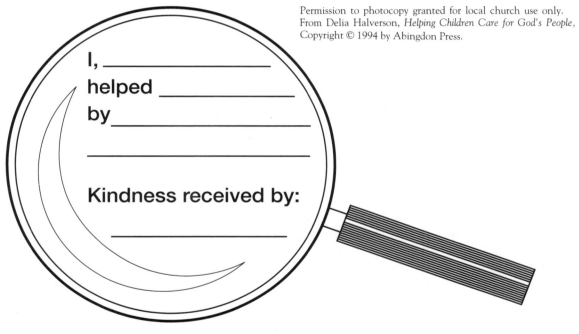

Stewardship of a Car

Although elementary children are too young to drive, their activities and demands often affect the use of the family automobile. Early development of a good understanding of stewardship in the use of a car will make a difference in their attitudes when they do begin driving. The idea for this activity comes from a curriculum for youth, *The Stewardship of a Car*, by Frankie Garrick, published through the South Carolina United Methodist Conference in 1986.

Divide the class into groups of 3-5 persons. Give each group a large piece of newsprint and markers, and ask them to fill the newsprint with drawings or words that give reasons for using an automobile. When all groups have finished, list the reasons under the following categories: transportation, symbol of power, status symbol, freedom, pleasure. Discuss the following:

- the reasons listed in each area, and whether these reasons are needs or desires.
- how each reason affects the family finances.
- how each reason affects the time schedule of individuals in the family (particularly the drivers).
- whether one area of reasons should take priority over another, if the car cannot be used for all reasons.
- the definition of stewardship of money and time, and why this makes a difference in the demands that each of us puts on the use of a car.
- alternatives to using a car in each situation.

Interview Adults on Energy

Arrange for interviews with adults on the ways they save energy. The interview results may be done in written form, or on audio or video recordings.

Loving Acts Calendar

Prepare a week's calendar to be given to each child. On the calendar, children record loving acts that are done for them each day. Before sending these home, discuss different acts to look for, such as preparing meals, driving the child to a certain place or event, helping the child when his/her hands are full, helping with homework, and so on. Children return the calendars after a week, and the class discusses some of the loving acts they received. Celebrate these acts of caring and thank God for them, and for those who gave them.

Hands of Kindness

Draw an outline of a child's hand on a paper. When each child has a paper, ask the children to think of ways they can help at home or at school, and write one item on each finger. The hands will remind them to carry out these acts during the week.

Research Ethnic Heroes

Locate books at the library on ethnic heroes who exhibited Christian characteristics in their actions. You might consider Richard Allen, who helped form the African Methodist Episcopal Church and became its first bishop when African Americans weren't treated fairly in the white church. Or consider Sojourner Truth, an uneducated African American woman who traveled across the country, preaching about the love of God, and speaking out first against slavery and, then in favor of women's rights.

The research may be presented in the form of a small book, as skits, or even as articles in the church newsletter.

Quotes from People Who Had Been Starved

"I was so exhausted. I sat in a puddle of water and I took off my shirt to wash it. A man came and see me and said, 'You look like a ghost. You're only bone and skin.' I didn't say anything. When you're so hungry, you can't even smile."

—Somaly Hay (was age 15 in Cambodia)

"It hurt to my bones. I couldn't breathe. I got so dizzy. I couldn't see anything. I still have some pain in my stomach. My head still aches . . . When I eat food, sometimes I just want to continue eating it [even though] my stomach is already full. I'm thinking I'm lucky to have this food and I eat it all. I still feel the starvation from 10 years ago."

—Arn Chorn-Pond (was age 16 in Cambodia)

(Kaplan, Lisa Faye, "The Horror of Hunger," *Ft. Myers News-Press*, January 5, 1993)

Research Hunger and Starvation

In our well-fed society, we often use the term *starving* to indicate hunger. Most of us have no idea just how the starvation process occurs. Assign research crews to use encyclopedias and magazines, and report their findings to the class.

They are likely to find that starvation comes from medically acute malnutrition, a result of not having enough to eat or drink. In order to survive, the body first devours its fat, then its muscle. Muscles no longer cushion bones, hair becomes thin and falls out, skin peels, nails crack, and gums and joints bleed because of vitamin deficiencies. We lose our immunity to disease, and our brain cells die, taking away our ability to reason, even our ability to think of ways to obtain food.

Consider creating family meditations for Lent or some other season, with a daily Bible passage and two or three sentences of information on hunger.

Brief Fast

Send home with the children a sheet of paper containing the following information. Ask that they fill out the sheet and return it next week, when you will discuss their experiences together. Be sure that you also take part in the research.

- Choose a day.
- Have no snacks after school.
- Have no supper before 8:00 P.M.
- Before eating, write down what it felt like:
  —during the afternoon;
  —in the evening before eating.
- Write down what it felt like after your meal.

Research Ethnic/National Backgrounds

Poll the class for the number of ethnic/national backgrounds represented among their friends. They may need to ask their friends to check with parents about their backgrounds, recording it later on paper.

Research Water

Young children can research and list the ways we use water each day, then think of ways to recycle water in the home, such as watering plants.

You might make up a form to ask families to read their water meters daily, then look at the use and discover why they use more water on some days than on others. Discuss ways to cut down on specific water use.

Divide the number of gallons used per day in a family by the number of persons living in the house, and you will know how much is used for each person. Persons in semiarid regions of Africa use only four-fifths of a gallon per day.

Older children can find out how your city recycles water. They can also use encyclopedias and library books for further information. It might include the following:

- Water covers three-fourths of the earth's surface. Of all our water, 97.4 percent is salt water; 1.8 percent is frozen; and .8 percent is fresh.
- Watering the lawn averages 10 gallons of water per minute. Brushing teeth while leaving the water running can take 10 gallons. By cutting it off while brushing, you can save 9.5 gallons.
- It takes 1,000 gallons of water to produce an aluminum can. Recycling cans saves this water.

- People can live up to two months without food, but will die in three days without water.
- All water is recycled. What you drink today may contain a molecule that a dinosaur once drank.

Documentary Hometown USA

With cameras as simple to operate as they are today, this project can be carried out easily by most elementary, and even younger children, with the help of adults. Move about town, looking for the ways we show good and poor stewardship of nature. Take photos of the evidence and record locations. Then make up a documentary book to show your findings. You might also include some statement about how each example of poor stewardship can be changed.

Language Lab

Check your local library for language dictionaries, tapes, books, and resource persons. Research translations for common words in different languages. Following is an example from the Hindi language. The Hindi people of India greet each other by placing their hands together, as if in prayer, and slightly bowing their heads as they say *nuh muh stay*. They may close their worship service by shouting, *Yee-shoo muhsee kee jigh!*

Word	Hindi Word	Pronounciation
Peace	यीशु	Sah-lahm
Jesus	प्रेम	Yee-shoo
Love	नमस्ते	Praym
A greeting	सलाम	Nuh muh stay
Victory to Jesus	यीशु मसीह की जै	Yee-shoo muhsee kee jigh

(*Church Times, Grades 1-3* [Nashville: Graded Press, July 1989], p. 4).

Gifts for God

Give each child several pieces of colorful paper. On the papers, they write gifts of time that they can give to God. These might include service in the church, service to others, study of the Bible, and so on.

Fold each paper in accordion fashion. Then lay a pipe cleaner in the middle of the fold, and tightly twist the pipe cleaner once around the folded paper. Each "gift" is then twisted around the branch of a tree displayed in the classroom, or on a cross made of small branches.

Close with a prayer thanking God for the gift of time and dedicating these gifts of time back to God.

Research Product(s)

Select a product and research with encyclopedias in order to show how it comes into your home. EXAMPLE: Bananas go from owner/grower in another country, to picker, to packing company, to shipping company, to importing company, to wholesaler, to retailer, to us.

OR

Use the picture on the following page to discuss how we rely on other people in the world, and the conditions under which those people live.

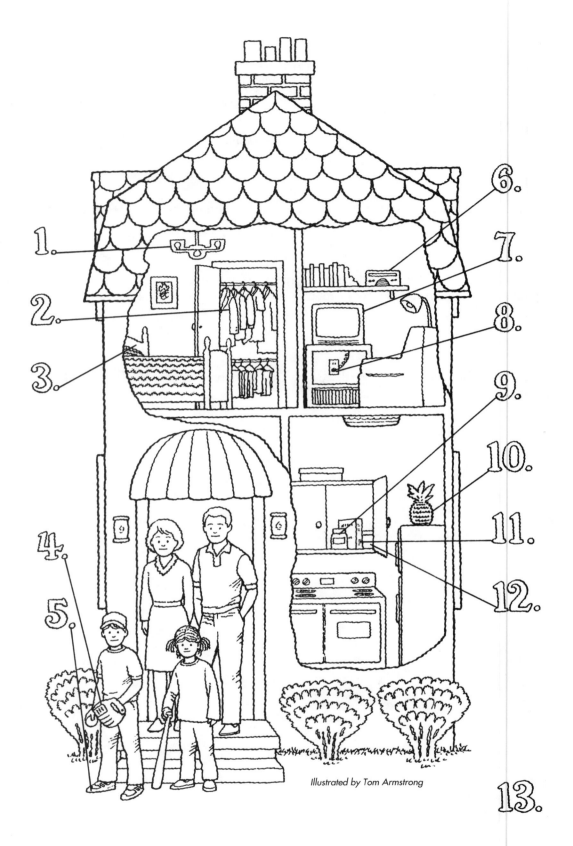

1.

2.

3.

4.

5.

6.

7.

8.

9.

10.

11.

12.

13.

Illustrated by Tom Armstrong

1. Filament for light from Bolivia. How many lights do you have in your house? _____ *A U.S. child will use 30 to 50 times more goods in a lifetime than one born in Bolivia's poor section.* What did you buy this year that you no longer use?_____
   Why don't you use it anymore? _____

2. Clothing from Costa Rica. How many shirts do you have? _____ *Workers in Costa Rica earn less than 40 cents an hour.* What do you do with the clothing you outgrow? _____

3. Teak furniture from Honduras. What furniture do you have that is made of teak? _____ *About 75 percent of the people in Honduras live in small rural villages and earn about $6.00 a month.* What did you pay for your last toy? _____

4. Baseball and glove from Haiti. Do you have a baseball and glove? _____ *In a Haitian village of 6,000 people, there usually are only two water taps. One out of every five babies born in Haiti dies before its second birthday.* How many children do you know under two? _____

5. Rubber in sneakers from Thailand. How many pairs of sneakers are there in your house? _____ *Most people in Thailand make $528 a year, or $10.15 a week.* How much allowance do you get a week, and how do you spend it? _____

6. Radio assembled in Taiwan. How many radios does your family own? _____ *Workers in Taiwan earn less than 25 cents an hour.* What did you last spend 25 cents on? _____

7. Parts of the television come from Burundi. How many televisions do you have? _____ *People in Burundi seldom live to be older than 42 years.* Do you know anyone who is about 42?_____

8. Electricity made from coal mined in Clear Fork Valley, Kentucky. How many electrical outlets are in your house? _____ *Two-thirds of the houses in Clear Fork Valley do not have flush toilets.* How many flush toilets do you have in your house? _____

9. Coffee from Guatemala. Who in your house drinks coffee? _____. *Two out of every three persons in Guatemala make only $42.00 a year.* What have you bought or been given that cost about $42.00? _____

10. Pineapples from the Philippines. Do you eat pineapples or drink the juice? _____ *Half of the children in the Philippines under four years of age are ill because they do not get enough protein.* Who do you know that is under four years of age? _____

11. Cocoa and fish from Ecuador. When do you enjoy cocoa? _____ Do you ever have tuna-fish sandwiches for lunch? _____ *In Equador, 60 percent of the children do not have enough to eat to keep them healthy.* What was the longest time you went without food, and how did it feel?_____

12. Sugar from the Dominican Republic. What foods that you like best contain sugar? _____ *Only 30 percent of the children in Dominican Republic ever live to be five years old.* Who do you know that is five? _____

13. Other common items supplied by poor countries: tea from Bangladesh; copper wiring from Chile; aluminum from Jamaica; tin from Malaysia; dog food made of fishmeal from Peru; cork (for bulletin board) from Algeria; natural gas from Mexico.

Teaching Through Games, Puzzles, and Paper

Games hold a rung near the top of the learning ladder. They give children opportunities to actually experience situations, and we learn best through experience. However, too often we think of competition when we think of games. We should not use competition as a motivational tool for learning. We should learn for the joy of learning. We can turn competitive thoughts into positive thoughts by stressing that we can put ourselves into the "shoes" or thought patterns of other people.

I have tried to include games that do not require expensive equipment or game pieces. By doing this we exhibit good stewardship. Talk with your children about using games that show good stewardship.

Be on the lookout for appropriate games in your curriculum. When you find one, don't let it go out with the trash at the end of the quarter. Use file folders with envelopes for the game pieces, or find a box for storage. You may even want to laminate the game at a local school-supply store, at a small cost per foot.

As you work with a game, allow the children to help establish part, or all the rules. This helps them learn to understand how different cultures arrive at doing things in certain ways. Acknowledge that there may be different ways of playing specific games, since common games sometimes have various sets of rules. Someone new in class may say, "We played it this way where I came from." Acknowledge this, and ask if others have played the game in other ways. Try several ways of playing, or several sets of rules, and affirm each one.

Puzzles attract some children, while others find them boring. I never enjoyed them much as a child, but as an adult, I find them challenging. Use puzzles for variety in your activities. Older children will enjoy creating puzzle games.

You will find two games from other countries at the end of this chapter, but I encourage you to research libraries for books that have more cultural games. Use them often, so that they become favorites with your class.

Add-on Picture

To play this game the "artist" draws a part of a picture on the board, and the class tries to guess what it is. After several guesses, the drawing is completed and becomes different from what most people thought it would be. Children may take turns being the "artist."

End by talking about how our ideas about something or someone are often prejudiced if we do not see the "whole picture."

Blocks and Rocks

Provide blocks and irregular rocks. On the blocks, write characteristics that promote peace; on the rocks, write characteristics that prevent peace. Ask the children to build a structure with the blocks and rocks. As you build, talk about how much firmer the structure is where the blocks are used, mentioning the characteristics written on the blocks. Also talk about how the uneven and irregular rocks can cause the structure to fall down easily. Talk about the negative characteristics on the rocks. After the experience, ask them how the experience of building with blocks and rocks was like bringing about peace.

Here are some characteristics you may want to use on the blocks and rocks:

Promote Peace	*Prevent Peace*
patient	demands own way
kind	always points out others' mistakes
forgets insults	not happy for others' success
forgiving	puts others down
shares	laughs at others
does his/her share	makes jokes at others' expense
speaks out when someone is wronged	lies about others
listens to others	never forgives

Caring Tag

This game of tag is played with two persons as IT. One person is the tagger, and the other is the care giver. When a person is tagged by the tagger, he or she must remain in the same position and not move until the care giver comes to give a caring tag—that is, a hug or a pat on the head. Play for a given number of minutes, then exchange and allow others to be the tagger and care giver. After the game, ask:
- How did you feel while you waited for someone to give you a caring tag?
- How did you feel after receiving the caring tag, and you were free to move again?
- How did you feel when you gave a caring tag?

Food-Chain Game

To prepare for this game, cut out several circles of colorful construction paper. Cut a slit about one-third of the way into each circle. On the circles, write items that make up various food chains. Here are a few, but you can research the library for others:

> acorn/squirrel/fox/bacteria
> mosquito/dragon fly/frog/turtle/human/bacteria
> lettuce/worm/robin/bacteria
> grass/cow/human/bacteria
> carrots/raccoon/vulture

The object of the game is to combine food chains by fastening the circles together at the slits. Many of these are cycles, particularly when you add bacteria to the chain.

Game Board

Board games may be used again and again, so your time in creating one will pay off in the future. On the following page, you will find a basic game board that you may reproduce. Children may help you create the game. If you mount it on a larger board or paper, they may also illustrate it.

To create your own game, decide on the theme. It could concern nurturing God's people, or it could be caring for God's world. Write positive actions on the subject in the squares that say "Go ahead" and negative actions, or obstacles, on the "Go back" squares.

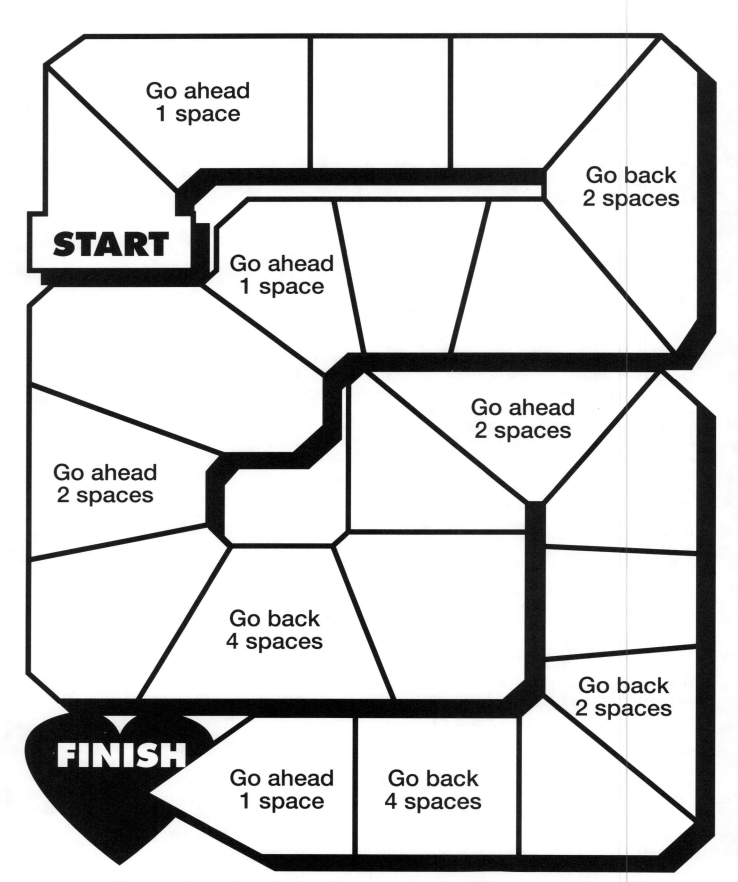

START

Go ahead
1 space

Go back
2 spaces

Go ahead
1 space

Go ahead
2 spaces

Go ahead
2 spaces

Go back
4 spaces

Go back
2 spaces

FINISH

Go ahead
1 space

Go back
4 spaces

If I Were

For this game, prepare identical slips of paper, each with the name or picture of a different item from nature. (Older children can help decide on items from nature and prepare slips ahead of time.) Place these in a basket or bag. Each child draws one slip of paper from the basket and explains what he or she would do to make God's world a better place for God's people, "If I were . . ." that item. After the game, you may want to make their statements into a poem or litany to be used in worship. Examples:

If I were a . . .	I would . . .
grain of sand	be a path for friends to walk on
cloud	rain on the food
lady bug	destroy bugs that eat the food
frog	eat mosquitos
worm	make the ground soft
squirrel	plant an oak
cow	give milk

NOTE: The same sort of game can be played by partners, the first person thinking of an "If I were . . . ." item, and the second person responding with "I would . . . ." Take turns as partners several times.

Jump In to Care

Children stand in a circle. Each child takes a turn giving a command, such as "hit your brother," "give half of your sandwich to someone," "ignore the poorly dressed girl at school," and so on. After each command is given, the other children decide whether the action is one that shows caring for God's people. For YES, they jump toward the center of the circle. For NO, they jump toward the outside.

Maze

Older children often enjoy mazes. Use a basic maze, such as the one on page 59 of *New Ways to Tell the Old, Old Story*, or make your own. At points on the maze, make pictures or write statements for your theme, which might be ways to care for God's people, or ways to have fun without spending money (which achieves your goal of stewardship).

Mobius Strip

The mobius strip may be made from long strips of construction paper or adding-machine tape. On one side of the paper, list people from various countries around the world (Filipinos, Japanese, Italians, etc.). If you have studied specific countries, use people from those countries. On the other side of the paper, copy this verse: "Whoever does not love does not know God, for God is love" (I John 4:8).

Hold both ends of the strip and make a half twist in the middle, taping the ends together. The Bible verse or names of people may be read by holding it loosely with the right hand and using the fingers of the left hand to pull it through the right fingers. Then turn it over to read the other side.

Puzzles

1. For this experience, purchase several small puzzles. (I usually place a colored dot on the back of each piece, using a different color for each puzzle. This makes it easier to assemble the proper pieces for each puzzle later.) Place a different puzzle on each table. Mix a few of the pieces from each puzzle, so that each table has a few pieces from other tables, but do not let the children know that there are mixed pieces. As they work the puzzles, they will discover that they must cooperate in order to complete the puzzles. Afterward, discuss how the children felt when they realized that all the pieces did not fit, how cooperation helped them achieve their goal, and how each person's actions affected others.

2. Or have everyone work on one puzzle together. However, ahead of time, remove a few pieces. As you complete the puzzle and realize that some pieces are missing, talk about how each piece is important to the whole puzzle and that each person is important to God.

Serving

Sit on chairs in a circle and bring out a tray with a variety of items (several more items than there are children, so that each has a choice). Items might include towel, spoon, ribbon, masking tape, adhesive bandage, piece of candy, glass, shoe, and so on.

Ask each child to choose one item and place it under his or her chair. When all have chosen, tell the children that a ball will be thrown across the circle to indicate turns. When a child receives the ball, he or she turns to the neighbor on the right, takes the item that is under that chair, and uses it in some way to serve the person in that chair. After serving, the child throws the ball to someone else, until everyone has had an opportunity to serve and to be served.

Afterward, say, "All of us have acted as servers and have been served. We are good stewards when we serve others. Jesus knew that it was important to serve, and he showed his disciples. This happened one day after they had walked a long way on dusty roads in sandals." Then read John 13:3-5, 12-17.

Ask: How did it feel when you served your neighbor? How did it feel when you were being served? What are some ways you can serve others this week?

Spending Time

Children need to have an understanding of time for this activity. Make 48 copies of the "time dollar" below for each child. Each child also will need slips of papers for the categories listed below, and any additional categories they may choose to include. The category slips will be laid out in front of the child. Each child decides how many half-hour increments he or she spends on each category each day. Then the child puts one time dollar below each category for each half hour they spend in that activity.

After all the dollars are spent, ask them to look at the way they are spending their time. Then suggest that they look at the categories and determine which time dollars they personally have the freedom to change, and consider changing them, if they feel they would practice good stewardship of their time by the change.

Example: If a child whose grades are not good is spending four "time dollars" (2 hours) watching TV, and only one "time dollar" (a half-hour) studying, then that child should consider increasing the time dollars for study and decreasing the time dollars for TV. Categories you might include:

dressing for school	visiting on the phone
going to school until return home	playing sports
homework	hobbies
watching TV	sleeping
visiting with family members	playing video games
helping with chores	helping brother/sister with homework

String Puzzle Hunt

This puzzle game may be used for various learnings, depending on what you choose to place on the cards attached to the strings. Children will work individually (or in small groups) to unravel a puzzle of string, collecting cards on their string as they go along.

To prepare for the game, make a set of 3 × 5 cards for each child (or group of 2 to 3 children). For each set, make one card for each of the following talents (or one card for each mission experience):

- Tell or read a story to a young child.
- Pick up litter.
- Listen to someone.
- Tell someone about your Sunday school class.
- Sing in the choir.
- Volunteer for a service project.
- Pray for someone.
- Help with a worship service in some way.

To lay out the string puzzle, secure the end of a ball of string to a door jam with tape. Unroll the ball, winding the string around and back and forth across the room, over and under furniture. Periodically, pin or tape one of the 3 X 5 cards (from one set) to the string. When all of the cards in that set have been used, cut the string and secure the end to some item with tape. Do the same with more string, so that each person (or group of 2 to 3 children) will have a string to follow, with a set of cards pinned or taped to the string.

Meet the students outside the door and wait until all have arrived before entering the room. Explain that you have laid out a string puzzle for them to follow. Give each person (or group) an envelope, a small stick for rolling the string, and the end of a string. Tell them that when you open the door, they should follow the string, rolling it up on the stick as they go, without breaking the string. As they come to the cards attached to the string, they are to remove each card and place it in their envelope. Tell them that this is not a race, and that they must cooperate with others, because the strings sometimes twist over each other. Then open the door and let them solve the string puzzle.

After solving the puzzle, talk about the items on their cards. Talk about how each person's string was woven across other strings and around objects. Talk about how all our lives touch one another.

Trade-About Game

To prepare, have identical sashes of two different colors, so that there are just enough sashes—half one color and half the other. Place each sash in a separate identical paper bag.

Children choose a bag and wait until all are chosen. Then, all at the same time, they remove the sashes from the bags and tie them around their waists.

Say, "Half of us are different from the other half. Hummm, I wonder which half is better. If you think the other half is better, you may find someone to trade with, but both of you must agree to trade." Set a time limit on trading, and let them move about, trading as often as they like.

Then ask: Why did you decide to trade? Why did you think your sash was/was not the best? (Some children may change because a friend had a different color or because they didn't like that particular color.)

Tell the story of Zacchaeus, and remind the children that Jesus didn't look at what others saw in Zacchaeus, but at what he was really like inside.

Water Jug Relay

Fill 10 one-gallon jugs with water. Divide into two teams, and give each team 5 jugs. Explain that in Kenya, 5 gallons a day is the amount of water each family uses. Remind them that this does not include water for lengthy showers, dishwashers, washing cars, or other uses.

Run a relay race, each person carrying all 5 jugs from one point to another. The winning team gets the privilege of using some of the water to make lemonade and serve everyone. Be sure that all leftover water is not wasted, but used in some way.

What's My Line?

Using the format of the TV show, three people come before the children, each claiming to be a missionary. Their clothing indicates other professions, but in their answers, they include the ways they are in mission (caring for others) in their own professions.

Woven World

Use construction-paper strips of various colors to represent the following:

green = trees/grass	blue = water
yellow = sunlight	orange = fruits/vegetables
tan = earth	purple = fruits/vegetables
gray = animals	pink = flowers

white/black/brown/red = people

As children weave the paper strips into a mat, discuss how each color represents a different part of God's world, and talk together about how anything that happens to one part of God's world affects all the other parts.

Games from Other Countries

Avo (African)

Avo is an old African game, now played in many parts of the world. Elaborate wooden avo games may be purchased, but one can be made from egg cartons. Tear off the lid of one carton, and break off two 2-cup sections from another carton for the "home cups." You will need 48 seeds or pebbles. Place 4 seeds in each of the 12 cups.

The game is played with two players, each player having two "home cups." The first player moves 4 seeds from any of the cups on his/her side and drops one in each of the next 4 consecutive cups. The other player does the same. Plays alternate, each player choosing a cup from his or her side and moving ALL the seeds, one by one, into the next consecutive cups.

If the last seed dropped lands in an opponent's cup that has fewer than three seeds, you then take all seeds from that cup and place them in your home cups. After your first play, you may move backward from the last cup in which you planted a seed, and collect seeds as you go along from cups that contain fewer than three seeds.

The game ends when one player has 24 seeds in the home cups, or when neither player can move again.

In this game, stress the joy of playing, rather than competition.

Mexican Piñata

Expensive piñatas may be purchased, but you can practice good stewardship and have just as much fun by making your own from a paper bag. The children can participate in making the piñata and double the fun!

You will need a large brown paper bag, tissue paper, masking tape, markers or crayons, colorful crepe paper, yarn, and a stick or broom handle; also, wrapped candies, small gifts, and other small favors and treats.

- Make stuffing for the piñata by wading tissue paper into balls.
- Fill the paper bag with the stuffing and treats, and tape the top shut.
- Paint or color designs on the bag.
- Cut crepe paper streamers and attach to the bag with tape.
- Attach yarn to bag and fasten to ceiling.
- Take turns hitting the piñata with a stick or broom handle until it breaks and scatters the goodies across the floor. For older children, you could blindfold the person with the stick, adding a challenge.

Teaching Through Music, Rhythm, and Readings

Music has passed from generation to generation in much the same manner as storytelling, and perhaps for as long a time. Rhythm may even predate music and seems to surge from the heart of our being. Readings combine tone and rhythm. When we celebrate with these methods, we make use of the gifts that God gave us.

Once children realize that they can manipulate their voice tones, they experiment with singing. This does not mean that they will always sing on key. In fact, some children sing off key with gusto for years, unless we show them how to listen to a note and move their voices up or down to hit that note. Therefore, do not assume that a child is tone-deaf until you have worked with him or her. You may suggest that children listen to the notes and move their voices appropriately, but I encourage you to leave the actual teaching of music skills to the school and private teachers. Recognize that we use music, rhythm, and readings as tools in Christian education. The experience creates the learning, and we do not aim for performance.

Although some of us feel uncomfortable leading in music, we need to include it in our tool chest as we work with children. You might engage someone else to help you with music in your classroom, or ask someone to help you make audiotapes of songs you want to use. But I would encourage you to experiment with leading, recognizing that you are not expected to "perform." Consider this a learning experience for both you and your class.

Children's Choirs

For children, a choir program should be learning-centered, rather than performance-centered. Encourage directors of your choir program to look for opportunities to expand children's understanding of care through the songs they sing. They might use songs from other ethnic and culture groups, and learn something about the people as they learn the songs.

Hymns and Songs

Look through your hymnal for hymns that carry the theme of our responsibility to God, to the earth, and to God's people. You may find these in the topical index, under such subjects as missions, outreach, love, peace, earth, nature, or stewardship.

Young children enjoy the song "We Are the Church Together." This song emphasizes the church as including ALL who worship Jesus, all around the world.

Be alert to popular songs that carry the theme of caring for others. Consider unique ways to adapt the songs to your use. For example, sing "He's Got the Whole World in His Hands," using peoples from different countries. Example: "He's got the Chinese people in his hands."

Discuss Hymns

Words act as the primary vehicle of thought as we sing our hymns. However, hymn singing in the church has become so routine that we seldom listen to the words. Before you sing, suggest that the children listen to the words, because you will talk about them afterward.

Example 1: After singing "Let There Be Peace on Earth," discuss three types of peace: (1) peace with self; (2) peace with family, community, or friends; (3) peace in the world. Ask: How do these build on one another?

Example 2: After singing "O Master, Let Me Walk with Thee," discuss: (1) *Master* is a term we sometimes use for Jesus; (2) How can we learn where Jesus wants us to walk with him?; (3) Where might Jesus lead us, if we really decide to walk with him?

Creating Songs or Hymns

Creating songs and hymns causes children to think about ways they can be stewards for God, and ways they can care. You might use some of the creation verses or scriptures mentioned in the first chapters of this book as a basis for your songs. Or you could make up phrases about stewardship and mission, following these steps to create songs or hymns:

1. Take one phrase at a time. Read or say it together for the "pulse" or rhythm.
2. Several students speak the phrase with the same rhythm. Listen to how some speak high, and some speak low. Refer to this as "color" sounds. Affirm uniqueness.
3. Listen again to the rise and fall and ask if any student will try to duplicate it with music. You may need to give a tone. Use the key of C and play C, E, G.
4. Sing the phrase several times, using the student's tune.
5. Move to other phrases, periodically repeating the whole song.

(From Delia Halverson, *How to Train Volunteer Teachers* [Nashville: Abingdon Press, 1991], Handout 19)

You may also use familiar tunes for your songs: "Oats, Peas, Beans, and Barley Grow," "The Farmer in the Dell," "Twinkle, Twinkle, Little Star." Try these lines to the tune of "Are You Sleeping, Brother John?":

> Je-sus loves us, Je-sus loves us,
> One and all. One and all.
> We are all God's children.
> We are all God's children.
> You and me. You and me.

Using the tune, "Did You Ever See a Lassie?" sing the following song:

Did You Ever See a Steward?

> Did you ever see a steward, a steward, a steward?
> Did you ever see a steward, do this and do that?
>
> Did you ever see a steward, a steward, a steward?
> Did you ever see a steward take care of God's world?
>
> Did you ever see a steward, a steward, a steward?
> Did you ever see a steward who messed up God's world?
>
> Did you ever see a steward, a steward, a steward?
> Did you ever see a steward of money and time?
>
> Oh, we are all God's stewards, God's stewards, God's stewards.
> Oh, we are all God's stewards, and you're God's steward, too!

(Sarah Fletcher, "Did You Ever See a Steward?" Copyright © 1984 Concordia Publishing House. From *Stewardship: Taking Care of God's World* [St. Louis: Concordia, 1984])

Sing this next song to the tune of "A Charge to Keep I Have."

A Charge to Care

A charge to care I have,
  A God to glorify,
Care for the world and all of life
On earth and in the sky.

A steward of the earth,
  Plants, water, creatures, trees.
My goal in life, my joy and love:
  My Lord and God to please.

I hear God's charge again,
  "See that my earth is kept."
Yes, Lord, I pledge my life to you,
  Your trust, I now accept.

Amen.

(From Delia Halverson, *New Call to Mission*, student book [Nashville: Graded Press, 1990], p. 8)

Talent Song

Each person thinks of one thing that he or she does well. Each time a child shares the talent with the group, sing a verse affirming that talent, using the tune to "Have You Ever Seen a Lassie?" *Examples*:

Mari-lyn trains the dogs,
  the dogs, the dogs,
Mari-lyn trains the dogs.
  We all give God thanks.

Ruthe-ford knows his ma-th,
  his ma-th, his ma-th.
Ruthe-ford knows his ma-th.
  We all give God thanks.

Sing in Different Languages

Locate or arrange for translations of common children's songs into different languages. Here are the Japanese words for "London Bridge Is Falling Down," translated by Masahiro Kasama:

Lon don ba shi o chi ta—o chi ta—o chi ta
Lon don ba shi o chi ta—Lon don ba shi.

(*Play! Think! Grow!* ed. Doris Willis [Nashville: Abingdon Press, 1992; trans. © 1992 by Cokesbury], p. 161)

Rhythm and Rap

Your children may be more experienced than you in developing rhythm or rap. Encourage them to work with you on the creation. Creating an expression of rhythm and rap may begin with the words, or with the rhythm. It is usually easiest to come up with one phrase that is repeated from time to time throughout the rap. Clap out the rhythm and listen to the phrase. You may need to change it in order to come up with an easy rhythm.

You might also check the hymnal for rhythms in familiar hymns, then work to fit words into that rhythm. Remember that this rap or rhythm is spoken without music. Here is an example, using the meaning of Matthew 25:31-46. Accent the words or syllables printed in bold.

Solo:	As **to** the **least** of **these** you **did,** you al-so **did** to **me.**
Group:	But **when** did we **see** you hun-gry, **Lord?**
	And **when** did we **see** you in **pain?**
Solo:	As **to** the **least** of **these** you **did,** you al-so **did** to **me.**
Group:	We **al**-ways **wel**-comed you with **joy.**
	We **don't** re-**call** you in **need.**
Solo:	As **to** the **least** of **these** you **did,** you al-so **did** to **me.**
Group:	You are **right,** our Lord, **we** were blind.
	For-**give** us, we **un**-der-**stand,**
	As **to** the **least** of **these** we **did,** we al-so **did** to **you.**

Choral Reading

Choral reading is done antiphonally (first one group or individual, then another). You may use poems, scripture, or hymn verses to create a choral reading. Look for pieces with phrases that sound both heavy and light. As you work with this, plan for the deeper voices or the whole group to speak the phrases that lend the heavier, or darker, feelings. Lighter phrases may be spoken by higher voices. This example is from Psalm 106:1, 3, 48.

Leader:	Praise the Lord!
Voice 1:	O give thanks to the Lord,
Voice 2:	for he is good;
All:	for his steadfast love endures forever.
Voice 3:	Happy are those who observe justice,
Voice 4:	who do righteousness at all times.
Group 1:	Blessed be the Lord,
Group 2:	the God of Israel,
All:	from everlasting to everlasting.
Leader:	And let all the people say, "Amen."
All:	Praise the Lord!

Create a Litany

In a litany, one or more lines are followed by a responsive phrase from the whole group. It may be a statement or creed, or it may be a prayer. The words of the litany may be said by everyone at once, or the sentences may be divided and read by different parts of the group.

You may want to set up the framework for a litany (such as the one below) and then have your class, or individuals in your class, complete it.

A Litany of Time

All:	We praise you, Lord, for the gift of time—
Voice 1:	time to be _____,
Voice 2:	time to do _____,
Voice 3:	time to help _____,
Voice 4:	and time to _____.

All:	We praise you, Lord, for the gift of time—
Voice 5:	time to think about _____,
Voice 6:	time to share _____,
Voice 7:	time to learn about _____,
Voice 8:	and time to _____.
All:	We praise you, Lord, for the gift of time. Amen.

(*Discover Fun & Fellowship* [Nashville: Graded Press, 1988-89], Discovery Sheet 5, Side 2)

Paraphrase

When we paraphrase, we put the scripture or other writing into our own words, rather than those of the author, but retain the real meaning. These paraphrases then may be set to music or rhythm, or used as readings by the group or by individuals.

After some practice as a class, older children can locate a scripture and work independently or in small groups. Young children need shorter verses and require more help. Proverbs 17:17a might be paraphrased in this way: *To be a friend, we always love.* Ephesians 4:32 could be paraphrased as, *Be loving to one another. Forgive one another as Christ taught.*

With older children, you might try paraphrasing in the reverse concept. If you do this, be certain the children understand that your purpose is to stimulate thought, and always compare the paraphrase with the actual scripture.

Compare the following negative paraphrase of the Lord's Prayer to the words that Jesus gave us. Talk about which words are selfish, and the way Jesus used words that showed he cared for others.

A Selfish Paraphrase of the Lord's Prayer

My Father, who provides for me. Hallowed be thy name. Thy kingdom come, thy will be done, if it doesn't inconvenience me here on earth. Give me today ten times the amount I need. I will eat it today and ask for more tomorrow. Forgive me, but take away the consequences. Don't worry about the others, for they surely caused their own problems! Lead me away from knowledge of how others are suffering. Let my eyes see no hard times that come to others. For you are powerful and can make me great! Forever! Amen.

Heritage Readings

Search the library for books of poems and readings. Using these not only helps children learn about caring for God's people, but it also lifts up our heritage of leaders in past generations. We recognize that people through the ages have cared for God's people.

Prayer of Saint Francis Assisi

Lord, make me an instrument of thy peace.
Where there is hatred, let me sow love;
Where there is injury, pardon;
Where there is doubt, faith;
Where there is despair, hope;

Where there is darkness, light;
Where there is sadness, joy.
O Divine Master, grant that I may not so much seek
To be consoled, as to console;
To be understood, as to understand;
To be loved, as to love; for
It is in giving, that we receive;
It is in pardoning, that we are pardoned;
And it is in dying, that we are born to eternal life.

                                                  Amen.

Using the thoughts in Saint Francis' prayer, lead your class in the following litany:

Group:	Lord, make us instruments of your peace.
Voice 1:	Where there is hatred,
Group:	Let us give love:
Voice 2:	Where there is injury,
Group:	Let us pardon;
Voice 3:	Where there is doubt,
Group:	Let us give faith;
Voice 4:	Where there is despair,
Group:	Let us give hope;
Voice 5:	Where there is darkness,
Group:	Let us bring light;
Voice 6:	Where there is sadness,
Group:	Let us spread joy;
Leader:	As we follow these ways, we will follow Christ. By following Christ, we bring closer the time when all the world will say:
Group:	"We live in harmony together, as God made us to live!" Amen.

Teaching Through Celebrations, Projects, and On-site Experiences

"But we're only children, and no one will pay attention to us!"

Such a typical statement! In fact, we adults often encourage such a statement with our own attitudes. Let me tell you about a group of fifth-graders in Saint Paul United Methodist Church in Atlanta who just didn't believe in such an attitude.

Class time was over, and the weary teachers weren't really sure the children had grasped the central thought of the morning. They had talked about our responsibility to care for the earth. As the children spilled out the doors, they headed for the fellowship hall and the refreshments shared by all ages between Sunday school and church. After a brief conversation concerning the morning, the teachers followed.

At the door to the fellowship hall, the teachers ran head-on into most of the fifth-graders, rushing out the door with styrofoam cups in hand. They approached the teachers with questions:

"Why do we use styrofoam cups at church? Shouldn't we be better stewards of our world?"

The teachers suggested that they talk with their parents during the week, and a couple of children were assigned to check with the church office about why they used styrofoam cups. They would all discuss it the next Sunday.

The class discovered that the church had no specific policy for types of cups, just that they'd always used this kind. Class members worked with the Children's Council to find a better way. They made calls to suppliers and discovered that styrofoam cups cost one cent each, while paper hot-drink cups cost eight cents each. The class knew that they must organize a good presentation to convince the church to switch. Another option was to use cups that could be washed and reused.

The children and adults spent several days preparing their presentation, collecting information about the pros and cons of styrofoam cups and the importance of the other options. They based their suggestions on the biblical concept of stewardship. As a result, the whole church's attitude was turned around! Now the church uses glasses and cups that are washed after each use. It can be done, and it can be done by children!

Celebrations and Festivals
Festival of Diversity

Plan an intergenerational, intercultural celebration to help your church family celebrate its differences and bring all ages together. Identify and invite persons of different ages and racial/ethnic backgrounds to provide leadership. Stress leadership from within your church, but include those outside the church too. The more leadership you involve, the more participants you will have.

Plan a two- to four-hour block of time for the festival, so that people can come and go at their leisure. Schedule and post the specific times that storytelling and other activities will be featured. Encourage everyone to come dressed in the clothing of their heritage. This is a project for all the Sunday school classes to work on together. Be sure the children help plan the event. Some suggestions: booths for crafts, storytelling, Bibles in various languages, food from different countries. Children love to dress up, so encourage them to come in garb that represents their heritage.

Festival of Friends

I must give credit for this format to Nancy Spence, Children's Director at Roswell United Methodist Church, and her able volunteer staff. Every third year, the children of Roswell, Georgia, and the surrounding area devote a concentrated week to growing in their understanding of friends around the world.

The children begin each morning in their assigned "Circle of Friends." At an appointed spot, they sit on a cloth circle and talk with their adult leader about specific subjects. During the remainder of the morning and early afternoon, the Circles of Friends visit various learning centers, where they learn about friends around the world by preparing foods, hearing and telling stories, playing games, learning music, learning about the geography and resources of various countries, dressing in the clothing and experiencing the arts and crafts of those countries.

Kwanzaa Celebration

Kwanzaa is a unique festival that celebrates the blending of African and American cultures. Although not uniquely Christian, the principles of Kwanzaa are easily incorporated into a Christian setting. It is celebrated from December 25 through January 1. For information and suggestions, see *Kwanzaa: An Everyday Resource and Instructional Guide* by David A. Anderson, and *Let's Celebrate Kwanzaa: An Activity Book for Young Readers* by Helen David-Thompson.

Mission Trip Celebration

Many churches now plan mission trips for youths and adults. Involve children in dedication services before people leave on a mission, and celebrations upon their return. You might also plan a celebration when professional missionaries come to visit.

Consider giving small towels to those participating in the celebration. The towels could be decorated with some symbol typical of the mission, along with the dates of the trip. Children could decorate the towels as their part of the celebration. Explain the towel and basin as a symbol for service, using John 13:1-20.

Taste of Our Heritage

Plan an all-church event, asking each family to bring a dish from their ethnic or cultural heritage. You may want to ask them to bring copies of their recipes, so that a cookbook can be put together afterward.

Prepare a large room or courtyard with several tables, labeled: appetizers, main dish, salads, desserts, and so on. Place a few chairs around the edge of the room, but do not place chairs at the tables. Purchase small paper plates, not the dinner-size. You want to encourage people to take small portions and move about the room, trying different dishes and talking together.

As families arrive, they write the name of their dish and it's ethnic or cultural heritage on a card, then place it with their dish on the appropriate table. Once everyone has gathered, say a prayer of thanks for the diversity of your church family and explain the procedure.

To enhance the event, provide background music from different heritages and close with several songs in a variety of languages.

Worship with an Ethnic Church

Most cities have several ethnic congregations. Arrange for the children to visit a congregation for a worship service. Afterward, talk about the common beliefs and practices, and how each church works to care for God's people.

Some churches adopt a church of a different ethnic background as a sister church. They then plan common worship services and fellowship times.

Worship with the Homeless

Homeless persons seldom feel comfortable attending a worship service where everyone dresses up. Some congregations, in areas where homeless people live, now plan informal worship services where they will be more comfortable. Check your community for such services, or plan to establish one through your church.

Church Street United Methodist Church in Knoxville, Tennessee, has established such a dress-down service on Thursday nights. College professors, third-generation homeless men, children with thrift-store shoes, and a bishop's wife now worship together.

(*Wesleyan Christian Advocate*, January 29, 1993.)

Projects and On-site Experiences

Adopt-a-Family

Look for opportunities to pair up families from your church with families from other churches.

Some of the families who lost all their Christmas decorations in Hurricane Andrew were paired with families from Grace United Methodist Church in Venice, Florida.

The families from Grace made duplicate Advent wreaths. They kept one for themselves and sent the others to their adopted families. The church also developed an Advent devotional booklet to go along with the wreaths, so that families in both churches used the same devotions during the season.

Bake Bread

Arrange with Meals on Wheels or a soup kitchen to bake corn muffins or another bread for a meal. Even young children can enjoy baking bread and helping to deliver the food.

Bike or Hike Sunday

Advertise churchwide that on a given Sunday, everyone is encouraged to bike or hike to church. On that Sunday, pin a badge on each person who biked or hiked, stating the miles traveled. Calculate the number of miles, and recognize the people and the number of miles during the service. You might also calculate the amount of fuel saved.

An alternative, if all your members live a great distance from the church, is a Carpool Sunday. During the service, recognize the families that carpooled to church and the amount of fuel saved.

Birthday for Missions

This could be an individual or a group project. Encourage children to ask that food, instead of toys, be brought to their birthday parties, and plan a trip to a local mission to deliver the food.

OR

Plan a Birthday for Jesus celebration. During the event, children (and adults) bring a gift (money or predetermined articles) to the front when their birthday month is called. This might be done at the same time as a children's choir program, with a birthday cake for everyone to enjoy afterward.

Blue-bag Lunch Special

Mount Blanchard United Methodist Church in Mount Blanchard, Ohio, planned to sell bag lunches to raise money for a mission project. In order to make their bags reusable, they came up with the following pattern for a blue-jean bag with two handles. They advertised their sales with a blue flashing light.

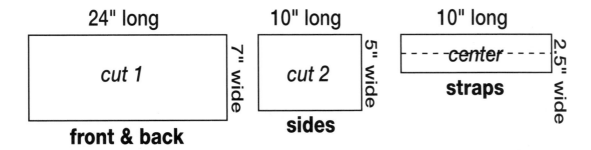

- Attach sides to front and back piece.
- To make straps, fold each side of strap piece into the center line, and fold again on center line. Then stitch.
- Stitch top of bag down to form hem.
- Attach a handle on each side of bag.
- Press bag.

(*Leader in the Church School Today*, Winter 1990-91 [Nashville: Graded Press, 1990], p. 21)

Calendar of Caring

Study twelve different mission/outreach projects in which your church participates. (Include projects sponsored by your church through your national body.) During the study, have children draw illustrations about each project. Then make calendars, using the illustrations and some brief printed information about each mission project. The children could write the dates and the names of the months on the calendar.

Arrange with a print shop to print and bind the calendar pages. If the print shop realizes that the proceeds will go to a mission project, they may give you a special rate. Then sell the calendars and give the proceeds to one of the projects.

OR

Draw up a calendar for the month. As a class, decide on specific thoughts or actions that might be printed on each day, as a suggestion for action during that day. Print the calendar and distribute it to families in the church. Some of the suggestions might include:

- Do you have records or audiotapes? Count them, and put aside five cents for each one for missions.
- Make a food gift for someone who lives alone and visit him or her.
- Count the number of items in your grocery bags this week. Thank God for your food, and give missions one cent for each item.
- Thank each family member for one thing he or she did for you this week.

Care Bears

Locate a simple pattern and make teddy bears (or other stuffed toys) or pillows for hospitals, nursing homes, and shelters for abused or homeless persons. Adult classes or women's groups might sew the toys or pillows, and the children could stuff them. Children and adults can work together in raising the money to purchase the fabric, and older children can help cut the fabric. If you work with adults, plan opportunities for them to work together with the children, or at least plan some activity together, such as delivering the gifts, to join in a celebration of your common mission. Children's experiences with other adults are as important as their experience with mission.

Care Packages

You may plan to put together care packages for various persons. Besides the usual packages for mission agencies, consider persons in your own congregation who are away from home—college students or persons in the armed services. Include such items as:

home-baked goods
photos of church activities
small banners with fun thoughts
sermon tapes

microwave popcorn
church bulletins/newsletters
fast-food restaurant coupons
devotional items

notes from the congregation, written earlier on 3 × 5 cards

Make this a total congregational project by purchasing the items ahead and displaying them on tables after a worship service. Then ask members to "buy" items to include in the packages. Have the boxes ready for packing, and when an item is "purchased," the purchaser can place the item in the box.

Care Quilts

After collecting money for the materials, children accompany adults to pick out fabric pieces to make quilts for individual needy families or children's homes. Young children can make cards to accompany quilts, and older children can cut the squares and tie the quilts.

Children of all ages can decorate quilt squares of light solid colors with fabric paints or fabric crayons.

Caring Tree

Use an artificial Christmas tree (or a large bare limb in a pot) as a collection point for gifts for a mission project. Ask the congregation to help trim (or "leaf") the tree with gifts. The gifts may be mittens, socks, school supplies, baby items, and such for community centers, abuse shelters, or other mission centers.

Collect for Others

Most churches have some sort of collection for the needy, but it usually becomes a routine procedure. Spice it up by designing a way to involve the whole church. Your class can sponsor it and advertise it throughout the church. Locate agencies early, to determine just what is needed. Divide the needs into groupings appropriate to ages, and distribute those lists in a creative way.

Some churches hand out "Bountiful Bags" in graduated sizes according to the needs, with the lists of needs attached. (They use grocery bags that have been decorated.) Others ask that the items be brought in shoe boxes. One church provided giant stockings to be filled at Christmas time.

Be creative with collection points. No one gets excited about dropping a can of soup in a plain cardboard box! Locate some "basement carpenters" who can make slatted wooden boxes for collection. Or decorate baskets and place them at strategic places about the church. You might set aside a specific Sunday and ask that the gifts be brought to the front of the church, as each family enters for the worship service. At Thanksgiving, create a huge basket or cornucopia for the collection; at Christmas, provide a specific tree under which the items are to be deposited. Celebrate, and make giving a joy!

Community Project

Children can care for God's people within their own community. Consider ways to care for the earth and for people in need. Clean up a vacant lot, plant trees, adopt a stream or road, or volunteer in an agency that helps homeless or abused children. Use Jeremiah 29:7 as you plan to help in your community.

Compost

Establish a compost box on church property for the entire congregation to use. Grass clippings, kitchen discards, and so on are worked into dirt. You might even rent or purchase a chipper for larger items. When the soil is ready, church members may come and take dirt for home use. Contact your local county Extension Agent for information on setting it up.

Creed-matching Deeds

With older children, go through the creed your church uses in your worship service, or your church's mission statement, and plan projects or personal deeds to carry out those statements.

Environment Friendly Display

Canvass local businesses and check in local stores to find companies that practice environmentally friendly policies. Prepare a display on a bulletin board or table with products in recyclable or refillable packaging.

Or gather information on companies that protect the environment, improve safety and morale conditions for employees, and help urban and community situations. Contact the advocacy group called Businesses for Social Responsibility for information on such companies.

Ethnic Stores/Restaurants

Spend some time shopping in ethnic stores, or plan to have a meal at an ethnic restaurant. Most grocery stores now display foods of other countries in a special area.

Field Trips

Plan a field trip that focuses on a specific tree, plot of ground, city block, or creek. Or you might visit parks, museums, parades, or ride on public transportation. Observe, observe, observe! Record (in writing or on tape) everything you see and hear. This might include conditions of nature, living conditions of people, whether the people are happy, and so on. Afterward, talk about what you have seen and whether the conditions are as God would like them to be. Consider ways you might help to change poor conditions.

Garden for the Hungry

Use a section of the church property for a garden, or arrange with someone in the church to use their vacant lot. Plant, tend, and harvest vegetables for a soup kitchen or to be distributed to the hungry. Or sell the produce and give the money to a mission project.

Love-in-Action Coupons

Make "Love in Action" coupons similar to the one below. Staple them together in groups of five, and hand them out to the congregation, encouraging individuals to fill them out and give them to others. Talk with your pastor about making this project a part of a Sunday worship which centers on caring for God's people. Place information about the coupons in the bulletin and newsletter.

LOVE IN ACTION

I, _____

**WILL PUT MY LOVE IN ACTION FOR YOU BY
(DEED)** _____

Signed _____

Mission Co-op

Work up a system whereby children may select small projects of service. These might include helping an older person with yard work, reading to sick persons, helping in the church office or nursery, or such things. Someone will need to coordinate the co-op by locating the projects, keeping records, then assigning the projects and following up. Be certain that recognition is given for those who participate.

Nursing-Home Visits

Nursing-home residents often spend lonely days, particularly between holidays. Many have few if any visitors, and very few have an opportunity to enjoy children. By making frequent visits to the same nursing home, children can establish lasting friendships with these adults. You might want to make cookies or some other treat, to take with you when you go.

Puerto Ricans traditionally visit nursing homes on Christmas Eve to sing Christmas carols. If you follow their example, point this out to the children.

Plant Trees

Tree planting can be as large or as small a project as you like. Write a litany to be used in worship in connection with this project. You might use Genesis 1:11-12, 29-30, or Psalm 1:3 as a basis for the litany. See TreePeople and the National Arbor Day Foundation in the Appendix, to write for more information.

To plant a *mini-forest*, you might find a farmer or landowner in your church or community willing to donate some land for tree planting. To obtain trees at little or no cost, call your local United States Department of Agriculture Soil Conversation Office, your local county Cooperative Extension Service, or The National Arbor Day Foundation (see Appendix).

What an example of stewardship a church could give by purchasing some property and beginning a *Confirmation Forest*. Each confirmation class could plant additional trees, and care for the forest would be an ongoing project for each year's class, throughout their study year. (See the story about Roger Baumeister below.)

Arrange with your grounds committee or trustees to *plant a tree at church*. This can be a project for children of any age, with the help of adults. You might involve parents in the planning and preparation for this project, and encourage families to plant trees in their own yards.

Plant a gift tree to acknowledge a marriage, anniversary, the birth, baptism, or confirmation of a child, or some other special event. Contact a local nursery about special prices.

Roger Baumeister

Share the story of Roger Baumeister with your children. Twenty years ago, Roger Baumeister bought 42 acres of land that had been stripped by mining and left ugly, eroding, and void of growth. He planted more than 75,000 evergreen seedlings and shrubs by hand—all purchased at a nominal fee through a state program. Today the six-acre pit lake that resulted from mining activities, plus the forest of new trees, attract rabbits, foxes, deer, quail, and even coyotes. The lake is full of fish and nesting waterfowl.

The Missouri State Park Board is so impressed by this man's success that it currently is reclaiming thousands of acres of stripped land for future recreational parks.

(*Older Elementary Student* [Nashville: Graded Press, Summer 1978], p. 53)

Raising Money for Projects

All projects cannot give on-site experiences. However, all of them can be visually appealing and involve active learning. A church in Tucson, Arizona, chose three exciting ways to promote its projects. When the children raised money for their Heifer Project, they made "chicks" of yellow pompoms, and glued on black paper eyes and an orange paper beak. These were put into plastic Easter eggs. Two nests were made of wood shavings, and the plastic eggs were placed in one nest. Each week, the children put their offerings into a hen-shaped basket, and when enough money ($1.00) was collected for one chick, a child was invited to open an egg and place a "hatched" chick in the second nest.

When they raised money for an infant nutrition program, they used a clear baby bottle to collect the money. Pictures of babies were posted, and a mother brought a baby to class for a visit.

A construction project that needed tools came to life with a house made of poster board, with small windows and doors that opened. The windows and doors were "boarded up" with brown paper, with a price printed on each. When an amount was raised, the corresponding door or window was opened to reveal the type of tool that the amount of money would purchase.

Other churches often use the idea of collecting pennies by the foot. Seventeen pennies make a foot. Calculate how many feet of pennies you will need for a specific project, and work toward that goal.

A church in Georgia collected money for tricycles for a Head-Start program. They made a large drawing of the parts of a tricycle (wheels, handle bars, seat, etc.), and as a given amount of money was raised, they added a part.

A Florida church purchased school supplies for a nearby mission. After each offering, supplies were actually purchased and placed at the front of the church. The children watched the mound of school supplies grow, and just before the beginning of school, several children went with adults to deliver them to the mission.

Be creative in your promotion of a project! Ask the children to help you think of new and different ways to display your project.

Recycle Shop

This can be done for a specific item or for all household items. Everyone who brings an item (such as a book or record) may take something home, or items can be bought for a nominal price. You might work out a means of trade, such as buttons that represent a certain dollar value and can be exchanged for something else.

Or you might simply come together as families and barter to exchange items. This takes less organization, and also results in verbal exchange between families. Insist that everyone recognize this as a way to act as good stewards, sharing those items no longer wanted.

Any money the project brings in can go toward a mission project.

OR

Bring discarded items, and then at a given time, come together as families and individuals to recycle the items by making something else out of them. Some examples might be stuffed toys from old jeans, scrap paper holders, pencil holders, vases, plant holders, and such.

Talents for Service

Youth programs often plan opportunities for church members to use the services of teens in order to raise money for a mission project. Why not set up this same opportunity for children? Here are some suggestions. You may come up with better ideas.

Plan an auction of talents. Set aside a time after church or during a church dinner, and have an auctioneer accept bids for services that children can provide. Another name for this auction might be Muscles for Missions. Avoid using the term "slave auction," so as not to imply sale of a person.

Why not barter for talents? The old art of bartering represents good stewardship. Exchange talents with others, agreeing to do a job or produce a product, in exchange for someone else's talent or product. This may be done at a church gathering or carried out through a bulletin board. Children and families can participate in this.

Create "wanted" posters for each child, including a photo and a description of a job the child will do for money to be given to a mission project. Post the notices around the church, with a space for adults to sign up for the child's service.

Set up a grass cutting/pet care/mail collecting service. Select a person to receive the calls and assign each project to a specific child. Help the children recognize that the time they spend on the project is their gift to God.

Yard Sale

Consider sponsoring a yard sale, the proceeds to go to a specific mission project. Ask the children to bring toys, books, and clothing to be sold. Emphasize the stewardship: of their talents as they prepare for and work in the yard sale; of their possessions as they are recycled for others to use; and of the money they earn for the project. Remind them that selling the items at a reasonable price allows those who cannot afford them to purchase the items. This is also a form of mission.

Event/Project Planning Sheet

Event/Project _____ Date(s) _____ Time _____

On church calendar?

Purpose _____

Participants (age, number, etc.) _____

Contact person/phone _____

Location/room set-up _____

Pre-event publicity _____

Post-event publicity _____

Supplies _____

_____

Refreshments _____

Expenses _____

Transportation/Drivers _____

  Directions: _____

Permission slips if necessary (Include emergency phone numbers, permission for emer-

gency medical treatment, and notary signature.) _____

_____

Outline/plan:

Follow-up plans:

Leaders/Helpers _____ Phone _____
                _____ Phone _____
                _____ Phone _____

Evaluation: _____

_____

Appendix

Caring Organizations

Children's Fund for Christian Mission, P.O. Box 840, Nashville TN 37202.

CROP (an ecumenical organization which provides food, seeds, tools, and various other kinds of appropriate technology)—Church World Service, P.O. Box 968, Elkhart IN 46515.

ECHO (Educational Concerns for Hunger Organization), 17430 Durrance Rd., North Ft. Myers FL 33917-2200 (813-543-3246). Uses volunteer help to research, develop, and distribute seeds and information on trees, edible plants, and small animals to deprived countries.

Friends of the Americas, an organization through which you may send a Christmas Box to children and families who live in deprived areas of Latin America. For information, contact Friends of the Americas, 1024 N. Foster Drive, Baton Rouge LA 70806.

Gleaning Network (includes Potato Project) Society of St. Andrew, State Rt. 615, P.O. Box 329, Big Island VA 24526 (800-333-4597). Program to glean fresh produce from fields that otherwise would be plowed under. (Some projects include families.)

Habitat for Humanity International (also Global Village Work Camp), 121 Habitat St., Americus GA 31709 (800-422-4828).

Heifer Project International, P.O. Box 808, Little Rock AR 72203. Assists poor families in rural areas throughout the world to produce more food and income for themselves with improved livestock. A notebook of stories, activities, and information is now available.

National Arbor Day Foundation, 100 Arbor Ave., Nebraska City NE 68410 (402-474-5655).

Potato Project. P.O. Box 329, State Rt. 615, Big Island VA 24526 (804-299-5956). This project salvages vegetables left in the fields after commercial pickers have finished. Because the picking is done through volunteer labor, the food can be delivered to the hungry for 1 cent per serving. You may purchase coloring books to advertise the project.

Save Our Streams (SOS) is a member of the Izaak Walton League of America, 1401 Wilson Blvd., Level B, Arlington VA 22209 (703-528-1818). They work to educate the public to conserve, maintain, protect, and restore the soil, forest, water, and other national resources.

Shoeboxes for Liberty, Friends of the Americas, 912 N. Forest Dr., Baton Rouge LA 70806.

TreePeople, 12601 Mulholland Dr., Beverly Hills CA 90210.

Trevor's Campaign (blankets for homeless), Trevor's Place, 1624 W. Poplar St., Philadelphia PA 19130 (215-236-4660).

UNICEF, 331 E. 38th St., New York NY 10016.

Resources
For Children:

About Caring and Sharing (Scriptographic coloring book on stewardship). South Deerfield, Mass.: Channing L. Bete Co., 1979.

Ada, Alma Flor, Janet Thorne, and Philip Wingeier-Rayo, *Choices and Other Stories from the Caribbean.* New York: Friendship Press, 1993.

Ashley and Adam (12-minute video with gender issues) New York: Friendship Press.

Barrett, John M., *It's Hard Not to Worry: Stories for Children About Poverty.* New York: Friendship Press, 1988.

Booth, Barbara, *Mandy* (a child with hearing impairment). New York: Lothrop, Lee & Shephard, 1991.

Brown, Marcia, *Stone Soup, an Old Tale*. New York: Charles Scribner's Sons, 1947. Other versions of this story emphasize the trickery by which strangers get a meal, but this one emphasizes the fact that if everyone shares, all are fed.

Carlstrom, Nancy White, *Grandpappy*. Boston: Little, Brown & Co., 1990.

Caswell, Helen, *God Makes Us Different*. Nashville: Abingdon Press, 1988.

Caswell, Helen, *God's Love Is for Sharing*. Nashville: Abingdon Press, 1987.

Children, Let Us Love (booklet with facts about food pantries, shelter, etc.). New York: Reformed Church in America, in cooperation with Bread for the World, 1992.

Coerr, Eleanor, *Sadako and the Thousand Paper Cranes*. New York: Dell Publishing, 1977.

DeGrote, Barbara, *Take the Pizza and Run*. Minneapolis: Augsburg Press, 1992.

DiSalvo-Ryan, DyAnne, *Uncle Willie and the Soup Kitchen*. New York: Morrow Junior Books, 1991.

Exley, Helen, ed. *What It's Like to Be Me* (written and illustrated about and by children with disabilities). New York: Friendship Press, 1984.

Farrell, Frank, with Edward Wakin, *Trevor's Place* (about a 12-year-old boy whose concern about the homeless began a blanket ministry). New York: Harper & Row, 1990.

Fletcher, Sarah, *Stewardship: Taking Care of God's World*. St. Louis: Concordia, 1984.

Fuentes, Vilma May A., *Pearl Makers* (stories about children in the Philippines). New York: Friendship Press, 1989.

GM Photographic, *I Need the Earth, and the Earth Needs Me* (video with children, emphasizing our responsibility for air, water, and soil). Most public schools have this, given by General Motors Photographic, 465 W. Milwaukee, Room B901, Detroit MI 48202.

Guthrie, Donna, *A Rose for Abby* (homeless theme). Nashville: Abingdon Press, 1988.

Hutchins, Pat, *The Doorbell Rang* (on sharing—age 2 and up). New York: William Morrow & Co., 1989.

Jackson, Molly, *We Thank God for the Clothes We Wear* (includes other cultures). Elgin, Ill.: Chariot Books, David C. Cook Publishing, 1991.

Jeffers, Susan, *Brother Eagle, Sister Sky* (interdependence of earth and creatures). New York: Dial Books, 1991.

Let's Learn About Stewardship (information and activities Scriptographic Book for older children). South Deerfield, Mass.: Channing L. Bete Co., 1979.

Life Stories (a game to develop intergenerational conversations). Golden Valley, Minn.: Limited Partnership, 1991.

Miles, Betty, *Save the Earth: An Action Handbook for Kids*. New York: Alfred A. Knopf, 1991.

Moore-Slater, Carole, *Dana Doesn't Like Guns Anymore*. New York: Friendship Press, 1992.

Our Global Village Series (on food, games, dress, instruments, etc. of many countries). St. Louis: Miliken Publishing Co.

Paek, Min, *Aekyung's Dream* (story of lonely Korean girl after moving to U.S.—Korean language on same page). Emoryville, Calif.: Children's Book Press, 1988.

Schell, Mildred, *The Shoemaker's Dream*. Valley Forge, Penna.: Judson Press, 1982.

St. Germain, Sharon, *The Terrible Fight*. Boston: Houghton Mifflin, 1990.

Skipping Stones (A Multicultural Children's Quarterly), P.O. Box 3939, Eugene OR 97403 (503-342-4956).

Summers, Stanford, *Wacky and His Fuddlejig* (factory worker substitutes a fuddlejig for war toys). New York: Red Ink Productions, 1980.

Vasquez, Ely Patricia Martinez, *La Historia de Ana (The Story of Ana)* (bilingual story of 12-year-old refugee). Carol Stream, Ill.: Hope Publishing, 1985.

Walker, Barbara, and Simms Taback, *Laughing Together: Giggles and Grins from Around the Globe*. Minneapolis: Free Spirit Publishing, 1992.

Wehrheim, Carol A., *The Great Parade* (stories of women from Old Testament times until today; includes many nationalities—with teacher's guide). New York: Friendship Press, 1992.

Wezeman, Phyllis Vos, *Benjamin Brody's Backyard Bag*. Elgin, Ill.: Brethren Press, 1991.

Williams, Karen Lynn, *Galimoto* (story of contemporary African village life). New York: Mulberry Books, 1990.

Wood, Douglas, *Old Turtle* (People cooperate to care for the earth.) Duluth: Pfeifer-Hamilton Publishers, 1992.

For Adults:

Beam, Cecile A., *Inviting Elementary Children: To Be in God's Mission.* Nashville: Discipleship Resources, 1988.

Englehardt, Carolyn, and Ruth McDowell, *Let's Join in Mission.* Nashville: Discipleship Resources, 1991.

Gaskill, Norma, *Inviting Elementary Children: To Be Stewards.* Nashville: Discipleship Resources, 1988.

Giving Beyond Living (Scriptographic Booklet). South Deerfield, Mass.: Channing L. Bete Co., 1974.

Halverson, Delia, *How Do Our Children Grow?* Nashville: Abingdon Press, 1993.

Halverson, Delia, *New Call to Mission* (adult/youth mission study). Nashville: Graded Press, 1990.

Javna, John, and the EarthWorks Group, *Fifty Simple Things Kids Can Do to Save the Earth.* Kansas City, Mo.: Andrews & McMeel, 1990.

Kemper, Kristen, ed., *Caring for God's World.* Prescott, Ariz.: Educational Ministries, 1991.

LeFevre, Dale, *Cooperative Sports and Games Book.* New York: Pantheon Books, 1978.

LeFevre, Dale, *Second Cooperative Sports and Games Book.* New York: Pantheon Books, 1982.

LeFevre, Dale, *New Games for the Whole Family.* New York: Putnam Publishing, 1988.

McGinnis, Kathleen, and James McGinnis, *Parenting for Peace and Justice, Ten Years Later,* rev. ed. (special chapter on stewardship/simplicity). New York: Orbis Books, 1991.

Make a World of Difference: Creative Activities for Global Learning, ed. Sandi McFadden, Office of Global Education. New York: Friendship Press, 1990.

Meagher, Laura, *Teaching Children About Global Awareness.* New York: Crossroad Press, 1991.

Millen, Nina, *Children's Games from Many Lands.* New York: Friendship Press, 1965.

SEEDS (magazine on hunger and poverty), P.O. Box 6170, Waco TX 76706.

Stewardship and You (Scriptographic Booklet). South Deerfield, Mass.: Channing L. Bete Co., 1974.

Stewardship of Time and Talent (Scriptographic Booklet). South Deerfield, Mass.: Channing L. Bete Co., 1979.

World of Children's Stories, included in The Children's World Series. New York: Friendship Press, 1993.

Curriculum:

Building New Community (God's Children Overcoming Racism)—(grades 4-8). Nashville: Cokesbury Press, 1992.

Gaskill, Norma W., *I've Got Something to Share!* (leader book with student leaflets for 6 sessions—grades 3-6). Nashville: Discipleship Resources, 1985.

Duckert, Mary, *Who Touched the Remote Control?* (TV and Christian choices). New York: Friendship Press, 1990.

Friendship Press (see address below) provides children's curriculum each year. These units focus on selected geographical areas or on specific concerns of the church in mission.

Oak Street Chronicles and the Good News (video-based study of Christian values—grades 3-4, adaptable for younger/older). Nashville: Graded Press, 1987.

Patterson-Samwalt, Susan A., *Stories for Sharing—Exploring Stewardship with Children* (parables dealing with stewardship, with study suggestions). Nashville: Discipleship Resources, 1993.

Send or Call for Additional Resource Ideas:

ACT (Action for Children's Television), 46 Austin St., Newtonville MA 02160.

Alternatives, P.O. Box 429, Ellenwood GA 30049 (404-961-0102). (Send for catalogue.)

Animal Town, P.O. Box 485, Healdsburg CA 95448 (800-445-8642). (Send for catalogue of cooperative games and activities.)

Bread For the World, 802 Rhode Island Ave. NE, Washington DC 20018 (202-269-0200).

Center for Global Education, Augsburg College, 731 21st Ave. S., Minneapolis MN 55454 (612-330-1159).

Children's Rain Forest, Monteverde Conservation League, P.O. Box 936, Lewiston ME 04240. (Buy protection for part of a rain forest.)

Church World Service Blanket Program, P.O. Box 968, Elkhart IN 46515. (Purchase a blanket for others for $5.00.)

Clergy and Laity Concerned, 198 Broadway, Room 302, New York NY 10038.

Co-op America, P.O. Box 18217, Washington DC 20036. (Purchase low-flow shower heads and toilet dams.)

Educational Resources, Church World Service, P.O. Box 968, Elkhart IN 46515.

Environmental Defense Fund (recycling) (800-CALL EDF)(800-225-5333).

Exitex Caribe, Inc., 2200 Post Oak Blvd., Ste. 428, Houston TX (713-850-7095). (Provide economical food for deprived countries.)

Federal Trade Commission (FTC), 6th and Pennsylvania Ave. N.W., Washington DC 20580 (regarding commercials).

Friendship Press, P.O. Box 37844, Cincinnati OH 45222 (513-948-8733).

Mail Preference Service, Direct Marketing Associates, 6 E. 43rd St., New York NY 10017. (to request name dropped from purchased mailing lists.)

Multicultural Program Materials Catalog, Chaselle, Inc., 9645 Gerwig Ln., Columbia MD 21046-1503 (800-242-7355).

Save Our Streams (SOS), Izaak Walton League, 1401 Wilson Blvd., Level B, Arlington VA 22209 (702-528-1818).

UNICEF (Write for catalogue. You might want to order the calendar of holidays all over the world.) U.S. Committee for UNICEF, 331 E. 38th St., New York NY 10016.